Unleashing the Free P

BITE-SIZED DOUG

By Doug Speirs

Winnipeg Free Press

I

Unleashing the Free Press funny man
BITE-SIZED DOUG

(c) Copyright 2009 Winnipeg Free Press
All rights reserved

ISBN 978-0-9682575-5-5
Printed in Canada

LIBRARY AND ARCHIVES CANADA CATALOGUING IN PUBLICATION

Speirs, Doug, 1956-
BITE-SIZED DOUG: unleashing the Free Press funny man / written by Doug Speirs.

ISBN 978-0-9682575-5-5
1. Animals — Humor. 2. Canadian wit and humor (English). I. Title.

SF76.5.S64 2009   C818'.602   C2009-902279-6

WRITTEN BY: Doug Speirs
PROJECT EDITOR: Julie Carl
ART DIRECTOR / PRODUCTION: Gordon Preece

III

IV

DOUG Speirs likes to make fun of his size — he's a big guy, so he stands out in a crowd.

But in the last few years, he's really become a lightning rod outside the office.

Wherever we go, from the local coffee shop to the fundraising gala, Speirs inevitably draws a cluster of fans.

"I love your column," they all tell him. "It's the best thing in the newspaper."

This does not go over so well with us serious journalists, who grimly set out daily to seek truth and justice for all.

But it makes Doug happy.

And I guess that's part of his charm. He's a very funny man who never lets the accolades go to his head.

It's not easy to write a humour column, (or at least, that's what he tells us) but three times a week in the *Free Press*, Doug manages to find a way to make us laugh. And that's a great gift in tough times.

I hope you enjoy this special "critter-themed" collection of In the Doug House columns. Many thanks to Art Director Gordon Preece, photographers Ruth Bonneville and Mike Aporius, copy editor Andrew Maxwell and Deputy Editor Julie Carl, for pulling it all together so well.

Margo Goodhand
Editor, Winnipeg Free Press

Doug would like to dedicate this book to his two dogs, but he won't, he says, because neither of them currently read his column.

V

CONTENTS

Unleashing the Free Press funny man

BITE-SIZED
DOUG

CHAPTER 1

Fear not, ladies
MOUSE-HUNTER MAN
TO THE RESCUE

E EEEEEEEEEEEEEEEEEK!
There's a mouse in this column.
More importantly, there may
be a mouse in my house. For the moment, at least, it's an alleged mouse
because I haven't actually seen it —
yet.

We were placed on DEFCON 1 (Maximum Force Readiness) a few days ago
when a high-pitched squeal erupted
from the den where my daughter was
watching TV.

Terror in her eyes, she sprinted into
the living room to tell me she had seen
a little furry shadow scurry across the
carpet and dart under the furniture.

The hunt was on.

3

I dragged the sofa and chairs away from the walls and inspected the carpet.

"If there is a mouse," I told my daughter, "it looks like he's been wearing your mom's slippers and leaving candy wrappers everywhere."

She was not impressed and vowed to move out and live with her friends, all of whom have fabulous rodent-free homes and fathers who routinely subdue wolverines with their bare hands.

The excitement was ratcheted up a couple of days later when another ear-shattering scream echoed through the house.

It was about 7 a.m. and when I dragged my sleep-deprived body out of bed and staggered into the kitchen, I found my wife — She Who Must Not Be Named — perched precariously atop a chair, a death grip on the front of her fuzzy red robe.

"I think I saw a mouse run under the fridge!" she squealed. "Get it!!!"

I should explain here there is a clear division of duties in our house — my wife is responsible for all bee- and spider-related emergencies, while I am expected to handle mice, birds, home invaders and telemarketers.

When I saw her on the chair, however, I said something clever, like: 'Ha ha ha. You look funny.'

Big mistake. My wife advised me to get down on the floor pronto and start rooting under the fridge or she would either divorce me or kill me, she just wasn't sure which.

Thinking quickly, I retreated into the bedroom where the dogs were sound asleep on our bed, oblivious to the high drama playing out in the kitchen.

I grabbed the wiener dog and, banking on its rodent-hating instincts, plopped it in front of the fridge. It took one sniff, then ran over to my wife and demanded to be let up on the chair.

I'm guessing this must be one big mouse.

So, it was off to the local Canadian Tire outlet, where I asked a sales clerk to direct me to their most powerful anti-mouse devices.

"That's the most popular aisle in the store right now," the beaming clerk said. "Winnipeg must have an infestation. I'm from Kamloops, and we don't have mice there."

After making a mental note to move to Kamloops, I perused an impressive selection of weapons.

We're talking everything from glue boards to snap traps to little battery-powered electrocution chambers. There are even "ultrasonic" repellers that use high-pitched sound waves to drive mice away or, I assume, render them deaf, making it easier to sneak up on them.

"If there is a mouse... it looks like he's been wearing your mom's slippers and leaving candy wrappers everywhere."

I needed expert advice, so I called Don Poulin, president of Poulin's Pest Control Services.

"There's not a day that goes by where we're not doing a mouse job," Don told me. "Every year is a little worse than the year before. Now, with this early snowfall, very few predators can get at them under the snow and they can multiply."

Seeking sympathetic ears, we took our tale of mouse misery to some friends, who listened patiently, then passed on an even more terrifying close encounter.

One of our friends was enjoying a Sunday walk in the woods a while ago with his daughter when he felt just the slightest tickle on his pants leg. After the walk, they drove to church and, in the middle of the sermon, our friend felt another tickle, this time on the seat of his pants.

"I turned around and looked behind me," he recalled. "I thought it was just kids, but there was no one behind me."

Then, there it was again, just the faintest little movement. Placing a hand firmly over the spot in question, he duck-walked to the side door of the church and slipped outside, where he shattered the world record for unbuckling his pants.

And, you guessed it, out jumped a mouse, no doubt gasping for a breath of fresh air.

Meanwhile, the waiting game continues. My house is adequately protected, but now I'm not sure what to do about my pants.

I mean, where do you set the trap?

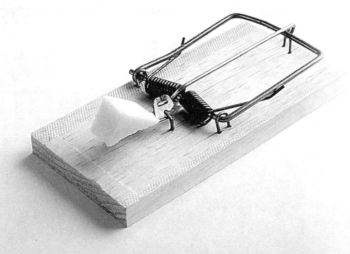

7

CHAPTER 2

Using my powers FOR GOOD, NOT EVIL

THIS is going to come as a major surprise — I am not your typical, off-the-rack superhero.

No, your traditional superhero is someone along the lines of Iron Man or, Spider-Man your basic troubled billionaire industrialist with a heart of gold or an angst-filled teenager with rippling abdominal muscles.

I'm more along the lines of the late actor George Reeves, who starred in the black-and-white TV version of Superman when I was a kid. I truly believed George was Superman, despite the fact he clearly spent waaaay too much time at the all-you-can-eat buffet and his supersize stomach left his stretchy pyjama-style costume on the verge of exploding. I suspect the only time he used his "heat vision" was to zap hotdogs when he wasn't standing around, hands on hips, deflecting bullets with his super-flab. Imagine an older Elvis with a red S on his chest instead of a white jumpsuit.

But getting back to me. My superpowers consist mainly of:

a) **the power to tear open a full bag of Cheetos using only my bare hands**
b) **the ability to empty a room of teenagers simply by asking if they feel like cleaning the garage**
c) **using a regulation TV remote control to flick through 375 channels in under 30 seconds**

Given these skills, you can imagine how excited I was when I was invited to portray an actual superhero in a photo shoot for a series of newspaper ads. These ads are for the Winnipeg Humane Society and are intended to promote Adopt-A-Cat Month, which happens to be June.

I was talked into this by Aileen White, the society's outgoing public relations and communications manager, the same person who persuaded me to spend four hours dressed as Santa last Christmas having my picture taken with dozens of dogs, cats, guinea pigs and snakes.

> **Confronted with the first cat they'd ever seen, my dogs reacted like a group of Boy Scouts meeting their first supermodel — they knew they were supposed to do something with it, but they just weren't sure what**

Aileen felt I'd be a perfect superhero, even though I am currently bald (after shaving my head for a cancer fundraiser) and sporting a hideous Frankenstein-style boot (because, for the second time in eight months, I've torn an Achilles tendon).

"What is not superhero-ish about you?" she said. "The idea of the ads is: You don't have to be a superhero to save a life! If we got a model to do it, they'd do the whole model thing. You're the Everyman."

"You mean, I'm fat," I said.

"No," Aileen beamed, "You're brawny."

Anyway, the big photo shoot took place at my house Monday and, because the whole idea is to get people to adopt cats, Aileen brought along an actual cat named Stormy to pose in the photos with me.

Stormy is an exceptionally mellow cat — he is the Bob Dylan of cats — and his job at the animal shelter is testing dogs to see how well they get along with cats.

Now I happen to own two dogs — a basset hound and a miniature wiener dog — both of which have brains the size of Raisinets and neither of which had ever met a cat face-to-face. My dogs believe their sacred duty is to stand at the front door and bark whenever anyone tries to come in because chances are they are:

a) bad people
b) edible

Confronted with the first cat they'd ever seen, my dogs reacted like a group of Boy Scouts meeting their first supermodel — they knew they were supposed to do something with it, but they just weren't sure what.

So the basset hound, after satisfying itself the cat was not edible, lost interest and instead attacked and devoured a sandwich my son had unwisely left undefended on the front table. The wiener dog, on the other

11

hand, bravely yapped at the cat from under our dining room table.

Being the size of a convenience store, I learned it was not easy to track down a superhero suit for the photo shoot. Mine consisted of a red-satin pirate-style shirt, a pair of billowy, bright yellow genie-style pants, a canary-yellow cape, and a fire-engine red headscarf.

Given the colour scheme, I looked like Hulk Hogan crossed with a giant bottle of French's mustard. In superhero terms, I was part pirate, part florist. But the shoot, under the guidance of photographer Frank Adam of Adam York photography, went surprisingly smoothly. Stormy was a real pro, and I didn't do too badly either, right until the point I discovered my newest cat-induced power — super-sneezing.

But that's not the main point. The main point is you animal lovers definitely need to go to the Humane Society right away and adopt some cats.

"We've got way too many cats," Aileen told me. "We get three times as many cats as dogs. There's a ton of cats and kittens up for adoption."

Here's my super-promise: If enough cats do not get adopted, I will come to your homes and personally demonstrate my amazing powers.

You're going to want to hide your Cheetos!

13

CHAPTER 3

Last one out
PLEASE
TURN OFF
THE PIG

T HERE'S no easy way to say this, so I'll just blurt it out — we've lost the race to develop the world's first glow-in-the-dark pig!

Sorry, there's just no way to sugar-coat a major scientific setback like the one we've just been handed by a group of scientists in Taiwan who apparently have way too much time on their hands.

Don't get me wrong, we've got a lot to be proud of: a) we're the greatest hockey-playing nation on Earth and, b) we pretty much rule when it comes to maple syrup.

Sadly, however, it seems we're getting our scientific butts kicked around the block in the brave new world of fluorescent pigs. (I can hear your collective gasp of despair).

15

This is especially galling in Manitoba, where I'm pretty sure we probably have more pigs than Tim Hortons outlets, if you can imagine that.

The glaring swine crisis came into focus this week after Taiwanese researchers — I swear I'm not making this up — successfully engineered pigs that glow fluorescent green in the dark.

They did this, according to news reports, by injecting genetic material extracted from jellyfish into the nucleus of cells in pig embryos.

"There are partially fluorescent green pigs elsewhere," a delighted Prof. Wu Shinn-Chih of National Taiwan University's department of animal science and technology told Ananova.com.

"But ours are the only ones in the world that are green from inside out. Even their hearts and internal organs are green."

Think it's not easy being green? Think again.

Even in daylight, the researchers say, the pigs' eyes, teeth and trotters look green and their skin has a greenish tinge.

But it's at night when they show their true colours. Make that colour.

But why, you may be wondering, would anyone want to have a green-glowing pig?

The Taiwanese scientists claim these green porkers represent a major breakthrough in the study of human disease.

The theory is that the fluorescent cells will show up during stem cell treatment of diseased organs, allowing physicians to more easily monitor the healing process.

That's what they say, of course. As a journalist with a long and glorious history of covering major pig-related stories, I have serious doubts.

It doesn't take much imagination (fortunately for me) to come up with a few potentially lucrative uses for such brilliant beasts:

16

1 CHRISTMAS LIGHTS —
This would seem to be a natural, even though they only come in one colour and you'd probably have to get a really, really big tree

2 HALLOWEEN DECORATIONS —
Another natural, but I'm thinking it would be pretty hard to keep them out of the kids' candy. Hey, they're pigs

3 PORCINE PATIO LANTERNS —
What better way to brighten up a summer barbecue. I suspect, however, they'd get more than a little upset if you grilled pork chops

4 AIRPORT RUNWAY MARKERS —
This would seem to be a good fit for rural airports, but it might be somewhat confusing for pilots trying to land at night if the runway started wandering around the field for no reason

5 NIGHTTIME TRUFFLE HUNTING —
OK, this might not be such a big hit in Canada, but imagine how popular it would be in France

6 NIGHT LIGHTS —
This has potential as long as you don't mind a source of illumination that continually squeals and smells like... um... a pig

"...ours are the only ones in the world that are green from inside out"

17

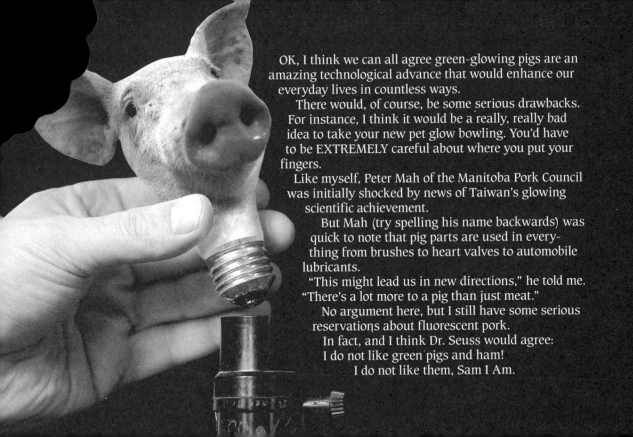

OK, I think we can all agree green-glowing pigs are an amazing technological advance that would enhance our everyday lives in countless ways.

There would, of course, be some serious drawbacks. For instance, I think it would be a really, really bad idea to take your new pet glow bowling. You'd have to be EXTREMELY careful about where you put your fingers.

Like myself, Peter Mah of the Manitoba Pork Council was initially shocked by news of Taiwan's glowing scientific achievement.

But Mah (try spelling his name backwards) was quick to note that pig parts are used in everything from brushes to heart valves to automobile lubricants.

"This might lead us in new directions," he told me. "There's a lot more to a pig than just meat."

No argument here, but I still have some serious reservations about fluorescent pork.

In fact, and I think Dr. Seuss would agree: I do not like green pigs and ham!

I do not like them, Sam I Am.

"There's a lot more to a pig than just meat"

CHAPTER 4

Here comes the champion
M-O-O-O-V-E
OVER

FROM the moment I first saw Diana, I knew we'd make an unbeatable team.

I'm not sure why I felt this way, given the fact we actually have so little in common.

For example, she's barely five feet tall, while I'm a towering six-foot-four.

She really doesn't say a word, while I tend to blather on forever.

She has huge liquid-brown eyes; my squinty peepers are steely blue.

She's a strict vegetarian; I'm an unrepentant carnivore.

She has four stomachs; I, sadly, have to make do with just one.

And she's a cow, whereas I'm a humour columnist.

21

Despite our wildly different backgrounds, Diana and I were able to come together for one magical moment at the 43rd annual Manitoba Stampede & Exhibition in Morris.

What I'm trying to say — and I don't mean to sound boastful— is that I was crowned CHAMPION at the rodeo's first-ever Milking Competition.

This thrilling victory came as something of a surprise, considering the closest I'd been to a cow before is buying ground beef at Safeway.

In hindsight, I credit this stunning upset to two critical factors:

1) I trained intensely, including tracking down a host of important cow-milking tips on the Internet

2) I cheated

Yes, you heard me, I am pretty much the bad boy of the competitive milking world.

But we'll get to that later.

The point is, I was part of an impressive herd of journalists who gathered at the stampede to get a grip on a fully functional cow.

Given the disintegrating situation in the Mideast, you'll be pleased to hear the milking contest was overflowing with reporters.

Seriously, had you been struck dead by a killer comet from outer space, you wouldn't have received half the media attention given to this confused cow.

I began my quest for gold by using a standard journalism technique — I asked the bartender in the VIP lounge for tips.

"Oooooh, let me tell you," Curtis Evenson beamed as he doled out cold beer "You can't just squeeze; you've gotta get a rhythm — kinda squeeze and let go, squeeze and let go!"

Armed with this invaluable information, I joined my fellow competitors under a blazing sun outside the dairy barn to meet Diana, a four-year-old 1,700-pound Holstein from Saskatchewan.

With the competitive fires burning hot, we besieged Diana's owner, Calvin Fornwald, with hard-hitting journalistic inquiries.

"Any milking tips, Calvin?" we yelled.

"Yes," the soft-spoken farmer replied. "Use a machine."

OK, score one for Calvin.

"How many Ns in Diana's name?" we demanded.

"How many would you like?" he drawled.

But my purpose here is not to complain about the secretive, high-pressure life of the competitive milker.

No, my purpose is to remind you, in big block letters, that I AM THE CHAMPION AND YOU ARE NOT! NEENER NEENER NEENER!

Sorry, but I've never won anything before, which brings us to this whole "controversy" over me being a big fat cheater.

You see, when my turn came, I drew a complete blank on every single milking tip I'd been able to round up.

As the TV cameras whirred, the only thing in my mind — I'm not lying here — was that scene from *The Karate Kid* in which Mr. Miyagi slaps his hands together and heals Daniel-san of athlete's foot. Or something like that.

So, after rubbing my mitts to make them nice and warm, I grabbed Diana's dangly bits with both hands and began tugging away with all my might.

We had 60 seconds to get as much milk in

"You can't just squeeze; you've gotta get a rhythm — kinda squeeze and let go, squeeze and let go!"

23

the bucket as possible.

"Look, I'm using the rhythm method!" I yelled at the swelling crowd of onlookers.

"CHEATER! CHEATER! CHEATER!" they yelled back at me. "You're supposed to use ONE HAND!"

Due to the fact there wasn't any instant replay — or any prize to speak of — the judges decided not to disqualify me.

Which means I have an entire year to milk my dubious achievement for everything it's worth.

But I'm not sure whether I'll defend my crown next year.

I think I speak for Diana when I say all the excitement has left us totally drained.

"Look, I'm using the rhythm method!"

24

CHAPTER 5

PLEASE BEAR WITH ME
...hey, I'm not kidding!

AS a seasoned outdoorsman and person with a beard, I am often approached by people who want to know how to handle an encounter with a bear.

After giving the question serious consideration for several seconds, I always give them the same advice: "By telephone."

That's exactly what my wife and I did the other night when the phone rang just as we sat down to dinner.

It was our daughter calling from somewhere near Canmore, Alta., where she's hiking in the Rocky Mountains with a bunch of high school classmates.

"Hi, honey, how's the trip going?" my wife asked as I sat listening and politely stuffing my face.

After a few meaningless "uh-huhs," my wife suddenly made what I would technically refer to as a Frowny Face and gasped.

"OHMYGAWD!" my wife said.

As a modern parent, I strongly suspected this was a clue something out of the ordinary had occurred.

27

> **I immediately adopted a look of great concern, then reached for the mashed potatoes**

"OHMYGAWD!" my wife said again.

Without regard for my own safety, I immediately adopted a look of great concern and reached for the mashed potatoes.

"It's your daughter," my wife said, pointing at me in case I might mistakenly think she was referring to someone else's daughter. "She ran into a GRIZZLY BEAR!"

Hearing this, I immediately flew into Parental Overreaction Mode and began screaming the first thing that popped into my mind.

"TELL HER TO STAY CLOSE TO EMILY!!!" I yelled, adding much-needed emphasis by pointing at my wife with a large piece of garlic bread.

Perhaps I should explain. What you need to know here is that Emily's father is an actual experienced outdoorsperson, whereas I am more of a "Holiday Inn" kind of guy.

As such, Emily's dad had the foresight to equip his daughter with something called a "Bear Banger," a device that apparently is a cross between a flame-thrower and a small nuclear weapon.

Anyway, our daughter and about 20 other young hikers entered a clearing recently and came within about 100 metres of a nasty-looking grizzly.

Initially, the bear began walking towards them but eventually wandered off, leaving the kids shaken but basically intact.

I should probably confess here that, as a well-known fraidy-cat, I rank bears somewhere between great white sharks and killer bees. Even at the zoo, I know the bears are sizing me up, licking their lips and thinking to themselves: "Yummy! I love the ones with the soft centres!"

But, as usual, this is not my point. My point is that we should all memorize a few safety tips during bear season, specifically:

1 If you insist on going hiking, remember you can't outrun a bear. This isn't a big deal provided you can outrun the rest of the people you are hiking with

2 It might not be a bad idea to hike with people who are heavier than you. I'm just saying

3 This may be pushing it, but it wouldn't hurt if some of the huskier hikers were covered in honey

4 In the rare case where the bear actually attacks, you should bravely grab the person next to you and yell out: "Here! Eat Murray!"

There might be a small problem if the person next to you doesn't happen to be named Murray, but remember... the bear won't ask a lot of questions

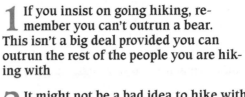

29

5 Always know the difference between a black bear and a grizzly. To do this, Internet experts advise you first climb a tree. If the bear climbs up and eats you, it's a black bear. If it shakes you out of the tree and then eats you, it's a grizzly

Anyway, until bear season ends, I think it is important that everyone within the sound of my voice try to follow these simple guidelines as closely as possible.

That's what my family has been doing and I am pleased to report that, as far as I can tell, none of us has yet been eaten.

So let's do our best to be careful out there, nature lovers. For the time being, remember to stick as close to Emily as you can.

And, please, whatever you do, don't let Murray out of your sight.

I personally will be at the Holiday Inn.

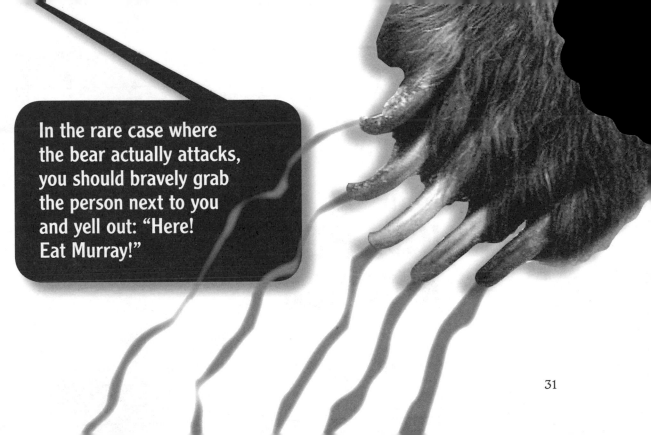

31

CHAPTER 6

The mouse came back...
NOW HE'S A GONER

'T WAS a couple of weeks before Christmas, when all through the house, not a creature was stirring...

Except for that stupid mouse. Oh, yeah, that little rodent was stirring all right. Stirring all over the place. Stirring up a big can of....

Sorry, I know it's the Season of Joy, but this story always gets me a little worked up. A few weeks back, I told you about an alleged mouse that had my family in a trap-laying frenzy.

Everyone was absolutely positive they'd spotted a furry little shadow scurrying around — everyone except me, that is.

Well, it's no longer an alleged mouse. In fact, it's now an ex-mouse. That's right, I'm a killer! A mouse-murderer. There, it's out in the open. I can feel the horrible burden of guilt beginning to lift.

And I know that you know exactly what I'm talking about here. Judging by the flood of emails after my first mouse-in-the-house column, half the city is doing battle with unwanted Christmas visitors.

A day or two after that column appeared, somewhere around midnight, our mouse tale reached its dramatic conclusion.

You see, my wife and I had just settled our brains for a long winter's nap, when out in the kitchen there arose such a clatter, I sprang from my bed to see what was the matter.

> "We locked eyes: His were beady; mine were bleary"

And there he was... dressed all in fur, from his head to his foot. Actually, he was sitting on top of the kitchen counter beside the fridge, casually checking to see if we'd left out any holiday baking.

We locked eyes: His were beady; mine were bleary.

Unfortunately, Squeaky had me at a bit of a disadvantage. When I sprang from my bed and ran into the kitchen, I did it without pyjamas or eyeglasses.

(Sorry to plant an image like that in your brain at this festive time of year.)

Even brandishing a broom, I was in no condition to do battle with a fully functional mouse. So I bravely screamed for my wife to join me, and bring my robe along with her.

Naturally, she refused. Instead, she opted to scream something incoherent and fling my ratty robe into the kitchen from about 30 feet away.

In the few seconds it took to make myself decent, the fast-thinking rodent ducked for cover. It appeared he'd made good his escape, until I spotted a teeny-tiny tail sticking out

> **...for reasons I'm still not sure of — I pointed at the mouse and screamed: "DON'T MOVE!"**

from behind a decorative ceramic tile leaning against the kitchen wall.

As I stood there pondering my next step — all the while pointing the business end of the broom at the tile — I was struck by an overwhelming sense of déjà vu.

(Cue eerie music... and begin flashback) It's December 1999, and I've just walked into the kitchen around 2 a.m.

My wife had warned me repeatedly not to leave any food out because she was certain we had a mouse. Of course, she ignored her own advice and left a freshly baked batch of chocolate chip cookies on the counter.

When I flicked on the light, I spotted a little brown mouse who was, at that very moment, in the process of helping himself to a cookie.

I looked at the mouse. The mouse looked at me. Our Mexican standoff lasted for what seemed like minutes until — for reasons I'm still not sure of — I pointed at the mouse and screamed: "DON'T MOVE!"

Ignoring my direct order, the mouse dashed away, dashed away, dashed away all along the counter and disappeared under the fridge, never to be seen again.

35

(Cue eerie music... and end flashback)

OK, I've spent about 20 minutes in my kitchen pointing a broom at our present-day mouse's hiding place.

Now don't get me wrong. I grew up watching *Born Free* and *Old Yeller*, so there's nothing I'd like more than to scoop the little fellow up, drive him out to the country and let him go spend the holidays with all his little mouse relatives.

But, as the flashback so painfully reminded me, I haven't had much luck persuading mice to surrender peacefully. And my wife WAS hiding in the bedroom demanding immediate — and preferably lethal — action.

I'll spare you the grisly details, but it turned out badly for the mouse... and even worse for the kitchen tile.

As for me, I'm having trouble sleeping. I keep dreaming of this miniature sleigh with eight really, really tiny reindeer.

CHAPTER 7

Swines!
Russian porkers
HOGGING
THE PIG
OLYMPICS

I was hoping I could make it until the end of spring without having to write another really depressing column about pigs.

But apparently, I was living a fool's dream.

You'll remember when I broke the tragic news that scientists in Taiwan had beaten Canadian researchers in the race to create the world's first glow-in-the-dark pig.

You'll remember this because it's exactly the kind of useless information that clogs up our brains and prevents us from remembering really important stuff, such as our phone numbers and our children's birthdays.

So you can imagine how excited I was recently when I learned that, cross my heart, the third Pig Olympics were to be held in Moscow.

I uncovered this major bit of sporting news after spotting a headline on a gripping Internet news story that boasted: "Russian piglets get ready for pig olympics."

According to news reports, this year's Games are shaping up as the most exciting ever and will see "athletes" compete in three thrilling events:

> "The piglets are being looked after by coaches and zoo psychologists"

1 **PIG RACING** — This apparently is all the rage in China and Russia, where special "Pigdromes" are popping up right and left so fans can watch speedy porkers huff and puff down the track.

2 **PIG-BALL** — Two teams of five piglets go snout-to-snout trying to push a ball into the opponent's goal. The piglets have to identify the members of their own team by smell, which I believe is how they do it in rugby and Aussie Rules football.

3 **PIG SWIMMING** — Just introduced for these Games, the races will reportedly be held in a specially built transparent pool. No word on how they'll get the pigs into their little Speedos.

Now, this is huge news for Manitoba, where we not only produce more pigs than potholes, but take pride in churning out record-setting Olympians.

Visions of little curly-tailed medallists dancing in my head, I called the Manitoba Pork Council to see how training was going for the porcine version of Team Canada.

And that's when my squeals of delight turned to gasps of horror.

Apparently — and you may want to sit down before reading this — there is NO Canadian team!

Andrew Dickson, the exceptionally nice general manager of the pork council, told me that, as far as he can tell, we're not sending any pigs to the Games.

"I think we have limited financial resources in this country, and we've been trying to focus on the human side," Dickson noted.

"In some places, pigs are pets and people do all kinds of crazy things with their pets."

Still, it's hard to believe we're leaving the field wide open for the Russians, who have launched an intensive training program so their porkers can own the podium.

It seems the Russians — and again I'm not lying — are using special coaches to hone their piglets' Olympic skills.

What? You think I'm exaggerating?

Consider this actual quote from Alexei Sharskov, vice-president of the Russian Federation of Sport Pig Breeders, who told Ananova.com:

"They are going through general training, and only after that will they take up different specialist sports.
"The piglets are being looked after by coaches and zoo psychologists."

That's right, we have real human athletes in this country who subsist on macaroni and cheese while Russian piglets get their superegos massaged by sports psychologists.

I'm not exactly sure what kind of issues Russian pigs have, but I imagine they're quite deeply rooted.

Russian sports psychologist: "Come in, Porkov. Please lie down on the couch and put your hooves up."

Russian sports pig: "OINK!"

Russian psychologist: "So, can you visualize yourself going for gold against capitalist pigs from inferior western nations?"

Russian pig: "OINK OINK!!"

Russian psychologist: "Very good, Porkov. Now tell me... Why do you hate your father?"

As it turns out, however, it's a very good thing that we aren't going to Russia with pigs.

This became clear after the pork council's Dickson explained that our "athletes" wouldn't be allowed back in the country.

"It would be a one-way ticket for any of the pigs that went because of the risk of dis-

ease," he said.

Ouch! Talk about bringing home the bacon.

As hard as this is to admit, I think for now it's best if we keep our pigs safe at home.

After all, there's no point going for the gold if your own government won't let you go wee, wee, wee all the way home.

43

CHAPTER 8

Burping cows **THREATEN PLANET**

BUUUURP...
excuse me

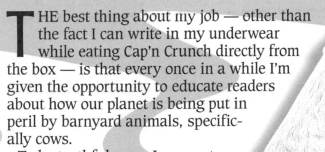

THE best thing about my job — other than the fact I can write in my underwear while eating Cap'n Crunch directly from the box — is that every once in a while I'm given the opportunity to educate readers about how our planet is being put in peril by barnyard animals, specifically cows.

To be truthful, even I was not fully aware of the extent of this global threat until last week when I stumbled across an Associated Press story with the provocative headline: "Swedish scientists study burping cows."

BUUURP... BUURP... excuse me

45

You will think I am making up this story, but I am not. Here is the very first paragraph: "STOCKHOLM, Sweden — A Swedish university has received $590,000 in research funds to measure the greenhouse gases released when cows belch."

And there you go! We are barely three paragraphs into today's column and already we have learned two stunning facts about Sweden that we did not know before we began thinking about it, specifically:

1) They have cows in Sweden
2) These cows burp

I am not an expert in bovine biology, but according to the part of this story that I believe I understood, cows generate huge amounts of methane when they digest food, meaning if they were to get bunged up, perhaps because of an improper diet, they could become "ticking time bombs."

This is why our government has to take immediate steps to prevent the forces of evil from getting their hands on even a single cow.

So my scientific point is that cows produce methane, which is a greenhouse gas, which contributes to global warming, which threatens the planet, which results in Al Gore making movies and a lot of long-winded speeches and winning the Nobel Prize, which is just wrong on so many levels.

According to this story, Swedish scientists want to feed a bunch of cows different diets, then measure the amount of methane the cows emit.

Now, you would think they would do this in the standard scientific manner, which is by hiring fraternity members to stand behind the cows holding large plastic bags. At least, this is how it was done when I was in college.

But you could not be more wrong. The story states — and get ready for a major scientific shock here — that 95 per cent of the methane released by cows comes out through the mouth.

So the Swedish cows are going to be outfitted with special burp-detecting collars that will measure the methane in the air around them.

This raises some troubling questions, including:

A) Just how hard is it for Swedish researchers to get dates?
B) Would: "Hi, I measure cow burps for a living," be a good pickup line in a bar?

And here's another shock: The head of the Swedish project claims, "This type of (cow burp) research is already being conducted in Canada, so we will be in contact with Canadian researchers in the near future."

As an investigative journalist, I knew I would have to determine the truth of that statement, provided it did not involve too many phone calls. So, I called the Dairy Farmers of Manitoba and conducted an actual "interview" with their general manager, a very friendly and helpful man named Brent Achtemichuk.

I hit Brent with a hardball question right out of the chute.

"Brent," I asked, "is it true that cows burp?"

"Yes," Brent told me.

"A lot?" I wanted to know.

"It depends," Brent replied.

Apparently, the amount of methane a cow burps up hinges on genetics and whether the cow is being fed a well-balanced diet overseen by a nutritionist, which Brent confirmed would rule out Mexican food.

> ## "Hi, I measure cow burps for a living"

"The amount of methane can vary from about 240 to 440 grams per day per cow," Brent explained.

More importantly, he also confirmed that actual Canadian researchers in Lethbridge, Alta., are right now monitoring burps emitted by Canadian cows.

He was unable, however, to confirm which end of the cow, methane-wise, is the most deadly.

"You've got me there," he said. "But I wouldn't want to be the researcher doing that; let's put it that way."

I also discovered Canada is making huge steps in curbing the amount of gas our cows burp into the atmosphere.

"Emissions from dairy cows have dropped 12 per cent between 1990 and 2003, and they continue to drop about one per cent per year," Brent told me.

Which makes us very proud to be Canadian.

That aside, there is a great deal more I need to say about Sweden and how our lives are being placed in jeopardy by cows, but that will have to wait until my next column.

For now, if you have any questions, you can reach me in the bar. There's a new pickup line I want to try out.

BUUURRRPPPP...

CHAPTER 9

Enjoy nature
WEAR
A HAT

IT'S Sunday evening and my heart is pounding so loud I'm sure it's only a matter of time before the neighbours phone the police with a noise complaint.

"THUMP! THUMP! THUMP!" my heart is going.

"ENOUGH WITH ALL THE THUMPING!" I'm pretty sure the neighbours are yelling.

My heart is hammering away like the drummer for Metallica because nature has decided to run amok in my backyard.

Here's the scene: I'm standing in one corner of the yard, our two dogs are snuffling in another corner, and Edgar is carefully perched in yet another.

Suddenly, the dense bushes in the only unoccupied corner, hops our nemesis — the Giant Killer Bunny Rabbit From Hell.

51

For a few tense moments we engage in a bizarre Mexican standoff, carefully eye-balling one another, anxiously waiting for someone to make the first move.

Finally, the bunny snaps and — I swear I am not making this up — begins a furious, headlong dash directly at Edgar.

This brazen assault prompts our bas-set hound, Cooper, who has roughly three functioning brain cells, to make a beeline for the bunny. Refusing to be left out, our sec-ondary dog, a miniature dachshund named Zoe, begins barking insanely and races after Cooper.

As a seasoned outdoorsperson, I make the only sensible decision — I fly into a full-scale panic and scramble after the dogs, screaming like a little girl.

Edgar's parents, who had been carefully monitoring the situation, now launch an all-out aerial attack on my head.

This is probably a good time for me to

mention that Edgar is a flightless baby crow that has been hop, hop, hopping around our backyard for the last five days.

While Edgar practises his takeoffs — it can take a young crow about a week to get off the ground — his parents have been resolutely dive-bombing us like tiny military aircraft.

Trust me, there aren't many things that can put a damper on a backyard barbecue faster than having your hair parted by an overprotective crow.

Anyway, Sunday's thrilling episode of *Wild Kingdom* ends when I drag the dogs into the house, the bad bunny bounces away and a terrified Edgar hides in a nearby bush.

But my purpose here is not to provide an informative glimpse into the wonder and majesty of nature.

My purpose is to strongly suggest that, if you are planning to visit my backyard while Edgar's parents are around, you really should wear protective headgear.

Specifically, I am thinking here of the kind of swell hats that my sister-in-law has been knitting and selling at a local farmers' market.

Technically speaking, the "hats" she has been knitting are, in fact, dog sweaters, but this distinction was lost on one of the customers who visited her booth this weekend.

Nice hat Doug...

"Nice hat," the would-be buyer exclaimed as she plopped the sweater on her head, "but the eyeholes don't line up!"

"That's because it's a dog sweater," my sister-in-law said.

"Oh!" the befuddled woman replied as she helped herself to one of the "cookies" on display.

"These are quite crunchy," the woman said.

"I hope so," my sister-in-law replied. "They're dog biscuits."

Meanwhile, back in my backyard, things seem to be going marginally better. Other than chasing away a bad bunny, the only help we've given Edgar is hoisting him out of a window well.

But the nice folks at Manitoba's Wildlife Haven Rehabilitation Centre tell me the best way to help a young crow is to leave him alone.

Lisa Tretiak, the centre's rehabilitation director, said juvenile crows usually spend a week on the ground learning to forage before they are able to fly.

If you do have to move a young crow because of imminent danger — cats, cars, deranged bunnies — Tretiak strongly recommends you cover your head.

Take it from me, a good crow-repelling hat is an excellent idea. And if you find yourself tripping over the patio furniture, try adjusting the eyeholes.

Five days and counting...

CHAPTER 10

NOTHING STIRRING,
especially
a mouse

I had just put the finishing touches on a column and was sauntering casually towards our front door when I saw the corpse.

He was pretty hard to miss, lying there like that, upside down on the little mat where everyone kicks off their mucky shoes and boots after walking into the house.

I was in kind of a hurry because I had promised to pick my daughter up after work and I was running late, so I almost tripped over the corpse when I went to put on my coat.

"GAK!" I muttered to myself as I stared down at the motionless body.

There's no question he was dead — his legs were sticking straight up towards the ceiling, his beady eyes were glazed over, and his tongue was lolling at an odd angle from the side of his mouth.

Still, being a professional newspaper columnist, I remembered what leading medical authorities advise you to do if you ever find yourself in a crisis situation such as this.

I quickly grabbed our fireplace poker and used it to jab the body several times. Yes, no doubt about it, this mouse was a goner.

What wasn't clear to me was how he got there in the first place. My 21-year-old son had walked past this very spot not 30 minutes before on his way to work, and I'm pretty sure he didn't mention anything about passing a dead rodent en route.

Mind you, it's possible he may not have noticed. When The Boy is thinking about cars or soccer or double-bacon cheeseburgers, he wouldn't notice a dead water buffalo or supermodel lying on the mat at the front door. I envy his ability to stay "focused" and "tune out" needless distractions.

As for the dead mouse, I'm sure the dogs had nothing to do with it. They'd spent the last couple of hours helping me write my column via the technique of sleeping on the couch while snoring and emitting potentially toxic vapours into the atmosphere around my computer.

No, clearly, moments earlier, this mouse had staggered into the living room and died, alone, of natural causes, which terrified me, because it means:

a) My house has become a retirement village for infirm mice
b) The mice in my house are gorging on so much readily available high-fat food that their cholesterol levels are skyrocketing, causing them to have fatal seizures as they attempt to waddle out of the kitchen

After giving the ex-mouse a decent burial, I tried to put the incident out of my mind. And I think I would have succeeded if it weren't for the smell.

It was a few days after the mysterious mouse death and I was happily driving along when it hit me — I'm talking here about the kind of smell that will snap your head back and make your eyes water.

It was coming from the area of my car where I assume the engine is located. It was the sort of fragrant aroma you'd expect if you tossed a dead skunk onto a bonfire, not that I have ever done this. I'm just saying.

Fortunately, when I got home, I knew just what to do. I asked my son to go have a look under the hood. This was not a hardship for The Boy. In fact, this is just the sort of situation he lives for.

In his mind, other than watching a Bruce Willis film festival, there's nothing in the world more manly than peering under a car hood, frowning at random engine parts, then shouting at someone to: "Try it now!"

I watched my son from a safe distance. "Is it the carburetor?" I asked. (This was a trick question because my wife has informed me that my car, in fact, does not have a carburetor.)

"No," my son said.

"Is it the battery?" I asked.

"No," my son scowled.

"Then what do you think it is?" I demanded.

"I'm guessing it's THIS!" he squealed with obvious delight as he held up the charred corpse of (surprise!) a mouse, which had apparently found a warm, if not safe, home on top of my car's engine.

Now, I'm not an automotive expert, but I am reasonably confident that car engines are not a natural environment for mice. They also should not be lounging around, dead or otherwise, on the mat at my front door. So I'm getting kind of worried. Especially because there's a strange smell coming from the toaster. I'm hoping my son will look into that real soon.

59

CHAPTER 11

Rootin' tootin' (doomed) COWPOKES

> **Did I mention I have never been on a horse? Ever? In my life?**

think I speak for tough-as-nails cowboys throughout this great manly land of ours when I issue the following deeply felt Old West-style sentiment: Yee-ha!!!

I base this sincere expression of unbridled cowpoke joy on the fact that, as far as I can tell at the moment, I am not currently dead.

The fact I am not pushing up daisies is somewhat surprising given that I agreed to take part in the big media challenge at the 44th annual Manitoba Stampede & Exhibition in Morris.

This year's "challenge" was barrel racing, which involves climbing on an actual live horse and riding at breakneck speed around metal drums in a figure-eight pattern in the centre of an arena.

This would be a good time to mention that I have never been on a horse in my life.

Here are some actual encouraging quotes from colleagues and family members after I told them I was going to try barrel racing:

"You are an idiot!"

"You are going to get killed!"

"You should chicken out, then write about that."

"Did I mention you are an idiot?"

I was able to put on a brave face, however, because I was pretty sure the nice folks who run the stampede probably did NOT want to upset members of the media by actually killing them.

What we journalists were expecting to ride was something along the lines of a nice, elderly pony, most likely blind and/or lame, with a soothing name like "Buttercup" or "Old Flannel Jammies."

Ha ha ha! I base that last outburst on the fact that we journalists were, in hindsight, idiots.

Our journalistic alarm bells began ringing when we arrived for the big event and organizer Arden Ross — sporting an authentic cowboy hat and a belt buckle the size of a canned ham — told us, and I quote: "It's going to be a real horse."

Did I mention I have never been on a horse? Ever? In my life?

> "You are an idiot'
> 'You are going
> to get killed"

64

So there we media types were, under a blazing sun, staring at not just a live horse, but TWO full-blooded Arabian horses and wondering which of us was going to get killed first and whether it would be polite for everyone else to film it.

Fortunately, before we got started, ranchers John Derksen and Kathy Bolduc, who supplied the horses — "Grey Sky" and "Brandy" — spent several valuable minutes explaining the operating instructions.

Always calm in the face of looming painful death, what I basically heard was this: "First you blah blah blah then make sure to blah blah and never ever blah blah blah!"

The part I did hear clearly was John making this soothing remark: "This is a dangerous sport, I gotta tell ya! Arabians are bred for war; they are the most hot-blooded horse there is."

The first obstacle to be overcome was deciding which "media celebrity" should go first.

The way we decided was by having the organizers yell, "OK, who wants to go first?" and then all the competitors (except me) yelled: "TAKE THE CHEATER! MAKE THE CHEATER GO FIRST!"

I should explain here that, technically speaking, the cheater was me.

This stems from the fact I won last year's big media challenge, which happened to be cow milking, by using both hands. Apparently international rules governing competitive milking state you can only use one hand. Who knew?

Just to be clear, going from cow milking to barrel racing is kind of like going from riding a tricycle to driving in a NASCAR event, if you get my general drift.

The next roadblock involved the appropriate method for getting a 270-pound person (this would be me) on top of a horse that clearly didn't even want a regular-sized person sitting on him or her.

In the end, it required TWO cowpersons to hoist me on top of "Brandy," a brown Arabian weighing about 1,100 pounds and standing "15 hands high," which is horse talk for "very big."

At this point, Kathy offered a helpful bit of advice, which was this: "Don't panic."

If you have ever had someone tell you this, you know that the first thing you do is immediately begin to panic.

"Don't boot him!" is what she said next.

"What???" is what I replied.

"When you want him to go, just give your legs a little squeeze."

"You mean like this... " was what I began to say when — and you will have seen this coming a mile away — Brandy took off like a (bad word) bullet fired from a gun.

What happened next was Brandy roared around the barrels like a (bad word) rocket while I held on for dear life and screamed some extremely uncowboy-like feelings at the top of my lungs.

As Brandy made the turn for home with me bouncing up and down like a 270-pound bag of Jello in an earthquake, a very important thought popped into my brain — I do NOT know how to make it stop!

"WHERE ARE THE (VERY BAD WORD) BRAKES!" I yelled as we raced towards the fence, behind which other media types were cowering.

And then the horse, apparently on autopilot, stopped. You will be pleased to hear I received thunderous applause.

As a general rule, media persons do not applaud other media persons. On this day, however, united by sheer terror, we applauded each other wildly to express our new journalistic motto: "Ohmygawd! You are still alive!"

Here's how race judge Peggy Penner summed up my ride: "You were quite the floppy wild man out there. You definitely need to improve your technique — and bring an extra pair of jeans with you!"

Later, a horse carrying plucky Citytv reporter Andrea Slobodian gave the distinct impression it planned to run right through the fence.

"Wow!" Andrea whispered moments later. "I was terrified. I thought we were going to crash into the judges' stands and then into the porta-potties."

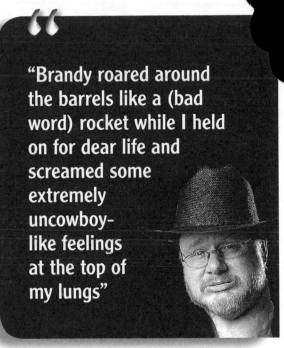

"Brandy roared around the barrels like a (bad word) rocket while I held on for dear life and screamed some extremely uncowboy-like feelings at the top of my lungs"

After her ride, normally fearless Shaw TV host Joanne Kelly put it this way: "It was truly scary. I jumped out of an airplane last week, and I'd do that again in a heartbeat. But not this!"

The big winner (in a time of 18 seconds) was my good buddy "Cowboy" Troy Scott from Hank FM. Troy, and this is clearly unfair, was raised around horses. Plus he has his own cowboy hat.

"My wasted youth finally paid off!" Troy beamed as he hoisted the winner's trophy. If you have to know, with a time of 35.5 seconds, I finished a painful seventh out of 11 entries.

But the best news of all, as I mentioned earlier, is the fact none of us was killed.

Mind you, we can always look forward to next year.

You're next, big boy

CHAPTER 12

Help, I'm being stalked
BY A BUNCH
OF WASPS

T'S a situation in which we all find ourselves around this time of year.

We are sitting out on the patio with a large group of friends, enjoying a cold beverage, savouring the warmth of a lovely end-of-summer day when, suddenly — this would also be without warning — along comes an uninvited guest determined to ruin our good time.

This obnoxious pest totally ignores our friends and instead zeroes in on us and, for no apparent reason, begins ramming himself into the side of our head and attempting to help himself to our tasty beverage.

As a calm, cool-headed newspaper professional, I always react the same way — I shriek like a little girl, wildly slap my head, then point at everyone else at the table and scream: "OH DEAR GOD PLEASE STING THEM!"

Because I really, really hate wasps. But, for some reason, they find me irresistible. I am not kidding. Trust me, if you were a wasp, you would be all over me right now.

The worst part is this: They have begun stalking me! I know this sounds a touch paranoid, but consider the evidence. In the last few days alone, rogue wasps have landed on and stung both my boss and my wife! Coincidence? I think not.

By targeting those closest to me, the city's wasp population is sending me an unmistakable message: "You're next, big boy!"

I know what you are thinking. You are thinking: "That is compelling evidence, Doug, but do you also have a Dramatic True Story about how you were personally menaced, if not actually stung, by a wasp?"

That is an excellent question and, fortunately, the answer is: Yes!

You will think I am making this up, but I am not. I was in my car the other day,

driving with all the windows open, partly because the sun was shining but mostly because I was singing along to *Radar Love* by Golden Earring and the radio was turned up so loud the sound waves needed an escape route.

And that's when a wasp flew directly in via my passenger window and slammed into my right ear, thereby rendering itself unconscious. Yes! Knocked completely cold. I know this because its tiny motionless wasp body plopped right onto my lap.

I do not know if you have ever driven for any length of time with an unconscious wasp a few centimetres away from your "medically sensitive region," but take it from me: it can be quite distracting.

The way I handled this situation was to glance down at the wasp, sweat profusely, then glance out the front window to find a good place to crash. The worst part came when, in between glances, the wasp van-

ished. Yes! Pfffft!
Disappeared.

Naturally, I assumed the
wasp had somehow found its way inside my
pants and I was about to suffer the Sting
Worse Than Death. But a few frantic moments later the revived wasp popped up,
gave me a chilling look and flew out the
driver's side window.

If this is not stalking, I am not sure what
is. Just to be safe, however, I decided to contact an expert. So I called the city's amiable
entomologist, Taz Stuart, and explained the
terrifying situation.

"I am being stalked by wasps," I told him.

"Ha ha ha," replied Taz, who is a very nice
guy and, along with being our city's top
bug expert, is noted for being a Tom Cruise
lookalike.

"Am I crazy or do wasps just like certain
people?" I asked.

"You're not insane," Taz said in an au-
thoritative and scientific manner. "You must
have sweet-smelling skin or something."

"Thanks," I said, trying to sound sincere.

"You're welcome," Taz said. "There's
something that makes you more
attractive. But if I sat beside
you, they like me, too."

"That's good to know," I told him.

"They think you might be a big flower.
If you are wearing bright-coloured clothing or a nice-smelling cologne, then, hey,
you are sweet and smelly and you might be
a food source. Then that one wasp tells his
neighbour and he tells his neighbour that
hey, this is a food source. Come and help us
take as much back to the nest as we can.'"

73

Taz and I talked about a bunch of other vital stuff, including the fact that a wasp scored a direct hit on his bicep recently when he was at The Forks competing in a dragon boat race.

Anyway, for the next little while we should all take a few simple precautions — only wear dark clothing and try to avoid smelling good.

Plus, if you have to sit outside, make sure you're with someone wasps find even more attractive than you.

I would recommend Tom Cruise.

CHAPTER 13

GIVE PEAS A CHANCE
— lettuce be friends!

SOMEWHERE BEHIND THE LINES IN MY BACKYARD — The war is not going well. The enemy has breached our last line of defence. I have been wounded. I fear the worst. AR-RRrrrrgh...

I hate to be melodramatic, but if my wife doesn't get back soon I don't think any of our tomatoes are going to get out of here alive.

It wasn't always this way. Earlier this summer, my wife, our commander-in-chief, was predicting victory in the War of the Tomato Patch.

It would be an understatement to say my wife is passionate about tomatoes — big, fat, juicy, red, sun-ripened, grown-in-your-very-own garden tomatoes. She defends her crop with the kind of wild-eyed, zealous, pro-tomato fanaticism that Osama bin Laden would probably criticize for being "just a little too intense."

The first assault of the summer came in the form of a bumper crop of tomato-starved bunnies. We easily have more bunnies frolicking in our backyard than Hugh Hefner could imagine in his wildest dreams.

But the garden general beat back the bunny brigades by ringing her future BLTs with an impressive mound of dirt and one of those cutesy little wooden fences they sell at home-renovation outlets.

But before she could taste the fruits of victory, a new, more insidious enemy surfaced, a long-eared, drooling beast driven by a savage, all-consuming hunger for tomatoes ripped fresh from the vine.

I am talking about our dog. Not our secondary mutt, a miniature wiener dog named Zoe, but our primary dog, a red-eyed, normally lethargic basset hound named Cooper.

You are likely thinking, based on those lovable mutts you see in the Hush Puppies shoe ads, that basset hounds are easygoing, non-threatening, wrinkled, sandbag-shaped sacks of waddling, drooling fun.

Ha ha ha! Let me just say, and I mean this in the best possible sense, you are a fool. When it comes to food, bassets are nature's Perfect Eating Machine, a land shark with a tongue Gene Simmons would envy and, despite a brain the size of a cashew, an impressive rat-like cunning.

It wasn't long before Cooper was

caught decimating the tomato plants, prompting my wife to erect a state-of-the-art anti-basset barricade — wooden stakes, chicken-wire fencing, old lawn furniture — around her tomatoes. Our garden is now more heavily fortified than the Pentagon. But that is not my point. My point is that my wife, She Who Must Not Be Named, deserted the battleground this weekend, fleeing to Calgary for a friend's 50th birthday, abandoning her family and her tomatoes.

And so there I was Saturday afternoon, sitting at the computer, partly searching for a topic for today's column but mostly staring at my left leg, which is encased in a big, ugly black boot, the kind of boot Frankenstein would refuse to wear on the grounds it made him look too dorky.

I am being forced to wear this high-tech, Velcro-strapped monstrosity and hobble around on crutches and a walker because I tore my Achilles tendon a couple of weeks ago in a charity baseball game.

Anyway, bored with my leg, I glanced out the picture window beside my desk and — RED ALERT! — discovered the basset hound had clandestinely tunnelled under my wife's defences and was gobbling tomatoes faster than Lindsay Lohan can suck down a shaker of cranberry martinis.

Able to do little more than shake my crutches in a menacing manner, I immediately launched the only weapon I had left — my teenage son, who ran howling into the backyard, chased Cooper out of the garden, around the yard, in the back door, through the kitchen and into the living room, where he (the dog) immediately jumped onto a comfy chair and began grinning at us with a weird chubby-cheeked Mona Lisa smile.

"He knows he's been a bad dog," I told my son in a fatherly tone.

"What are you talking about?" The Boy asked.

"Just look at that goofy smile on his face," I said. "He looks like a chipmunk on steroids."

"He's not smiling, dad!" The Boy insisted.

To prove his point, he walked over to the dog and gently hoisted up the drooping flaps on either side of its muzzle, revealing two smushed tomatoes tucked securely into either side of his red-stained cheeks.

And so the war continues. We don't have any carrots. The tomatoes are almost gone. And I'm trying to get the dog to sign a peas agreement.

I

Cooper

agree to
only...

**eat
peas**

81

CHAPTER 14

AN OPEN LETTER TO MY DOG
(the bad one)

To: My basset hound
Cc: My wiener dog

DEAR Cooper: I realize that, being a basset hound, it is highly unlikely you will actually read today's column, but at this point I've run out of ideas for communicating with you and am pretty much willing to try anything.

So, let's consider this an intervention. What I'm trying to say is your recent behaviour has been less than acceptable, not that your track record is anything to brag about.

Do I need to remind you about that Christmas fiasco? That's right, the time you found a 20-pound sack of flour in the kitchen, ripped it open, ate about five pounds' worth, then gulped down your entire water dish and rolled in the rest of the flour to ensure you were evenly coated in a thick, white, dripping mass of glue, which you then tracked throughout the living room while testing out the new leather sofa and every single chair to see which was the most comfortable.

But that's ancient history. I think we can agree things have been sort of going downhill from there. Just for fun, why don't we start with what you did in the living room yesterday?

Can you show me in the Official Dog Handbook the part where it says: After eating a bunch of grass and the remains of a dead squirrel, never throw up outside if there's a perfectly good carpet in the living room?

Hey, there's more to life than food! I'm serious. You can't eat everything.

83

For example, and this will be a big surprise, Kleenex, paper towels, discarded "hygiene" products, small pieces of wood and plastic bags from Safeway are not considered edible.

Do you have any idea how many fancy-schmancy, high-tech garbage containers we have bought in a vain search for one can — one (very bad word) can — that you CAN'T tip over or pry open on the off chance it might be full of yummy coffee grounds, eggshells or mould-coated things from the back of the fridge?

And do you really think we don't know what's been happening to the butter? Oh, yeah, like I really believe the kids have forgotten how to use knives and have been climbing up on the kitchen counter and using their tongues to lathe the butter into a disgusting, albeit very smooth, little blob.

Look, none of this would bother me so much if just once — one (very bad word) time — you would just look at me and say:

'Hey, my bad!' Or: 'Sorry, I just sort of lost control!'

But, NO! Whenever we catch you red-handed, you just sit there with that stunned ('Who? Me?') once-again-I-am-unjustly-accused look on your-droopy mug, as if butter wouldn't melt in your mouth (which it does).

And have you noticed how no one wants to take you for a walk anymore? Why? Because you don't walk. No, using the same gravitational pull as the space shuttle, you try to yank our skeletons out through our armpits. ("OHMYGAWD! LOOK OVER THERE! IT'S A SQUIRREL!")

What I want to know is why you can't be more like those dogs we see on TV. Not Lassie or Rin Tin Tin. I mean heroic dogs we see on the news, like that black Lab down in Maine who grabbed his owner by the arm last week and pulled him out of a burning house.

85

But you don't have time for stuff like that. You devote all your mental energy to breaking out of the backyard by ramming through rotten boards in the fence. The neighbours don't like that. They are cat people. Their cat hates you! That's why he hisses at you all the time.

(Just so you know, that fire that I mentioned a moment ago was caused — and I do not think The Associated Press would make this up — by a cat named Princess who tipped over a kerosene lamp. I'm just saying.)

You appear to have modelled yourself after Pepper, that Lab-shepherd cross in Wisconsin who, according to AP, got into his owner's purse and wolfed down $750. On the upside, the family — and they wisely wore rubber gloves to do this — was able to recover and wash off $647 that Pepper kindly "deposited" in their backyard, if you get my general drift.

Maybe I'm being a little harsh here; I don't think I'd be mentioning any of this if it weren't for that little incident with the wiener dog on Friday. You need to realize that you are roughly 10 times bigger than the wiener dog and, under the laws of physics, the two of you cannot occupy the same space at the same time.

That's why, when the two of you tried to run in the back door together, you managed to bodycheck the wiener dog off the top step, causing her to cartwheel in mid-air and land in the planter on the patio.

Not that you've asked, but, other than a slight limp, the wiener dog is going to be just fine. The vet bill, however, cost me $77. And guess who I think should pay for that?

If you're smart, I think you'll contact your buddy Pepper down in Wisconsin. I hear he's still sitting on a little cash.

P.S. Would you please stop licking yourself while I'm talking to you!

87

CHAPTER 15

AN OPEN LETTER TO ME
(from my dog Cooper)

I have been amazed by the size of the response to a recent column, in which I wrote an open letter criticizing my basset hound, Cooper, for his recent bad behaviour.

A large pack of readers on this continent and others — this is true, by the way — wrote in, some suggesting that, as responsible pet owners go, I obviously have all the intelligence of a chew toy.

(I suspect some of these may have been cat owners who appear to be growing increasingly restive — Note to self: Look up meaning of "restive" — over my "blatant anti-cat bias.")

But, floating among this sea of letters was one that literally jumped out and bit me in a medically sensitive area.

It was from my dog.

Ha ha ha! OK, I'm not joking here. Seriously, it was from my basset hound. The email address was my dog's name. I had no idea he knew how to use the computer, although this would go a long way toward explaining all that drool on the keyboard.

Here is Cooper's response to my open letter:

From: Cooper Speirs
To: Speirs, Doug
Dear Doug: First of all I must say I am somewhat disappointed that you chose such a public forum to air our dirty laundry, especially if you thought I wouldn't read your column. It makes me wonder why you wrote it in the first place. Was it to make me look bad in front of your fellow humans?

89

Let me respond to your misdirected frustration, and I say misdirected because as you'll read further it is not entirely my fault. But if you had walked a mile in my shoes you would have known that.

Since you brought up the Christmas incident, I clearly see that you don't appreciate my efforts to put a smile on your face. I can't believe you didn't think that was funny. I'll bet if you asked your readers you'd be hard-pressed to find one who didn't think it was funny.

But let's talk about the other day. Did it ever occur to you that I was trying to save the grass and the squirrel for later? Aren't you the one who said there's more to life than food? I was merely trying not to wolf down everything at once, but now you make it sound like such a bad thing. And you know I have a Kleenex problem I've been trying to shake for a while now; did you really have to bring that up? I thought we agreed to keep that between us.

That's just great. Is that what those fancy-schmancy cans were for? Keep things away from me? And all this time I thought you were trying to challenge me to keep my mind stimulated and sharp. I figured eggshells are good for my coat and a source of calcium, and the coffee grounds were just a test to see if I can sniff out the mouldy stuff underneath that I carefully display on the floor to draw to your attention that it's bad and needs to be thrown out.

Butter? Mmmm, butter...

That wasn't me.

Now let's talk about the walking. Do you know the effort and selective breeding it took to finally come up with such an exquisite breed like the basset HOUND, for the sole purpose of hunting pesky little critters like squirrels? And now you have the nerve to complain that I actually do my job well, and very enthusiastically, I might add. Do you actually expect me to ignore a squirrel when I see one? That makes no sense to me.

On top of all this you bring up the neighbours' cat? I don't trust that cat.

Do you know how many times I saw that cat snooping around the BBQ? But have you once — one (very bad word) time — thanked me for potentially saving our house from going up in flames?

$77? You expect me to cough up $77 for the vet bill? Did it ever occur to you or the wiener dog that being 10 times (aren't you exaggerating a little?) bigger that I would have the right of way? You always take the wiener dog's side.

I need to see a shrink, a Doggie Shrink (yes, he does exist... look it up: www. DoggieShrink.com), or I am going to lose it completely with all the mixed messages I get from you, thank you very much.

Sincerely,

Cooper

Anyway, I'm not sure what made me more anxious: the idea that my dog knows how to use a computer and can therefore tap into my bank account, or that someone out there actually took the time to create an email account in my dog's name.

Eventually, I clued in that Cooper's letter was written by "The Doggie Shrink" (a.k.a. Zoltan Hegyesi) in what I believe was a sincere and humanitarian effort to get some free publicity.

Zoltan, whose website boasts "a perfect dog in 60 minutes or it's free," told me a client had pointed the column out to him and just thought it would be funny to write a reply. So there you go.

Apparently my dog now has a shrink. A Fido Freud. Maybe it'll help Cooper work out a few issues. On the other hand, now that he's in analysis, I'll never get him off the couch.

CHAPTER 16

FINDING NEMO
in your toilet

IT'S 10 a.m. on a Tuesday morning, I'm barely awake, I haven't even had a cup of coffee yet, and I'm staring intently at Esther Nagtegaal's toilet.

I am staring at Esther's toilet with the kind of intense, all-consuming, passionate stare I normally reserve for staring at my television during Game 7 of the Stanley Cup final.

Before we go any further, I do not want to give you the wrong idea. As a rule, I do not make a habit of staring at the toilets of people with whom I'm not intimately familiar.

But, in Esther's case, I was willing to make an exception.

> It is not easy, using mere words, to describe the sense of inner contentment and calm you experience when sitting in someone else's bathroom watching four goldfish swimming around in their toilet tank...

I'll tell you why. First, Esther is an extremely gracious and elegant woman, the sort of person who is willing to invite a humour columnist into her home to stare at her toilet. She's a marine safety inspector with Transport Canada — in fact, she's a former ship's captain — but she looks like a fashion model.

Second, Esther has what I personally believe to be one of the most amazing toilets in the entire history of toilets.

Her toilet is not just a toilet; it's an aquarium. I am not making this toilet up. As a gift to herself this Christmas, Esther purchased the world's trendiest new bathroom fixture, which is something called the Fish 'n' Flush.

If you do not own one — and I find that difficult to imagine — the Fish 'n' Flush is a see-through aquarium that wraps itself around a clear inner tank. Happily, no fish are harmed when you flush.

It is not easy, using mere words, to describe the sense of inner contentment and calm you experience when sitting in someone else's bathroom watching four goldfish swimming around in their toilet tank, but I will try: It is very, very pleasant!

As we sit on the edge of her hot tub, Esther is politely explaining why she decided to transform her toilet into an aquarium.

"I just thought it was the most unique idea," she says. "It matched the nautical theme of our home, and I just find the fish very soothing.

"It's the most relaxing thing, lying in the tub and listening to the sound of the bubbles."

I should point out that I would not be in Esther's bathroom staring at her toilet if it were not for the vision of one man, an innovator named David Parrish who — and this is going to be a major surprise — lives in California.

David is the chief operating officer of AquaOne Technologies Inc., which specializes in water-conservation equipment for home appliances and often displays these devices at trade shows using clear acrylic tanks.

Now, David is definitely NOT the kind of guy who looks at a clear acrylic toilet tank and asks: "Why?" No, he is the kind of guy who looks at a clear acrylic toilet tank and asks: "Why not fill it up with a bunch of fish?"

And that's exactly what he did, giving birth to the Fish 'n' Flush, which was unveiled at a trade show in the mecca of all things tasteful, Las Vegas.

"We did it totally as a joke," David told me during a lengthy chat. "But the next thing we knew people were lining up to see it. We thought it was insane, but the response is really starting to snowball."

Since they began selling them on the Internet for $299 US, AquaOne has shipped more than 1,000 toilet-tank aquariums around the globe.

But the really exciting thing — and this is what makes our country so great — is that the Fish 'n' Flush has been a major hit in Canada.

"Canada is actually a bigger market for the Fish 'n' Flush than any single state in the U.S.," David said. "Canada is a little bit more open to new ideas."

A rather modest person, he couldn't help boasting the Fish 'n' Flush is the most revolutionary toilet-related development in memory.

"I think it's a product whose time has come," he beamed. "It's going to change the way people look at their toilets."

Which brings us back to Esther's bathroom, where I spent a great deal of time mesmerized by her toilet, of which she is justifiably proud.

As an investigative journalist, I felt com-pelled to ask a few hard-hitting questions, such as whether her friends and family think she's crazy.

She just laughed. "No one has said, 'You're absolutely nuts!' They just say, 'What a neat idea.' It's definitely a conversation-starter."

I couldn't help asking Esther whether I could put her toilet-aquarium through a trial run. She was much too polite to say no, but in the end I just couldn't... er... go through with it.

Call me paranoid, but I just had this strange feeling something was watching me. Even when I put the seat up.

CHAPTER 17

The blind woman and the
THREE-LEGGED DOG

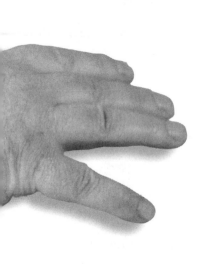

SINCE prehistoric times, humans have found one thing funnier than just about anything else — hearing about people getting maimed or killed in unusual and amusing ways. It's especially funny if the person getting maimed or killed doesn't happen to be you.

Science has proven that, for example, if someone is eaten alive by a boa constrictor while golfing or drowns in a giant vat of chocolate while touring the Hershey factory, there will be a little three-inch story about their demise in pretty much every paper in the world.

Newspaper editors think of these kinds of gruesome stories as brighteners.

This is because newspaper editors are the kind of people who believe trafficking in human misery is a great way to make friends and influence people.

So, they're pretty much like the rest of us. Which brings us to my very own, personal and (cross my heart) COMPLETELY TRUE tale of self-destruction. Let's call it the story of The Blind Woman and the Three-legged Dog, even though that pretty much gives away the best bits.

Now, you're probably thinking: "Doug, why should I care if you were eaten by a giant snake or set ablaze by a tribe of pygmies? "I don't know anything about you!"

By way of introduction, here are three fun facts about me:

1 I'm six-foot-four and weigh approximately the same as a small refrigerator, although not one of those stainless steel numbers

2 I have repeatedly been told I resemble...
a) legendary Winnipeg NDP MP Bill Blaikie
b) legendary Guess Who guitarist Randy Bachman and
c) legendary burger chain clown Ronald McDonald

3 I have memorized every single word of dialogue in *The Wizard of Oz* and *A Christmas Carol*.

I do, however, routinely forget my PIN number and I once briefly forgot my own name while introducing myself at a big journalism conference in Hamilton.

Now that we're acquainted, back to the story... this harrowing event occurred almost precisely one year ago as I write.

I was watching TV on a lovely Friday afternoon while my dogs — a basset hound with a huge appetite and a long-haired miniature dachshund with an even bigger attitude — were on window-monitor duty.

Suddenly, the wiener dog erupted in a

cacophony of agitated barking. It sounded something like this: "Ruffruffruffruffruffruffruffruff... grrrrrrrrrr!"

In wiener-dog-speak, this translates to something roughly like: "Hey, you in the blue Toyota, get off my street, or I'll track you down and nibble on your neck while you're sleeping."

With both dogs bouncing off the walls, I made the first of two near-fatal mistakes: I opened the door to get the mail.

As I rummaged in the mailbox, the basset hound thundered out the door with the wiener dog in hot pursuit.

Their plan was to greet a very pleasant-looking woman and her equally pleasant-looking dog standing innocently at the end of my driveway.

With my overly friendly pets bearing down on them, I did the only thing I could think of... I panicked and gave chase.

I do, however, routinely forget my PIN number and I once briefly forgot my own name while introducing myself at a big journalism conference in Hamilton

If you can picture it, at the end of my porch there is a very lovely trellis-thing made of wrought-iron leaves that supports the roof. This is where I made near-fatal mistake No. 2.

In my mind, I planned to wrap my arm AROUND the trellis and slingshot myself off the porch towards the fleeing dogs.

In fact, I stuck my arm THROUGH the trellis and, when I launched my body off the porch, my arm pretty much went the other way.

It sort of sounded like this: "CRUNCH! CRUNCH! CRUNCH!" I'm not a doctor, but, at the time, I realized my arm was not meant to be shaped like the letter S.

It looked not unlike a snake that had just been beaten to death with a nine-iron.

Thinking quickly, I called to the mystery woman at the end of the drive: "Ummm, I think I broke my arm. Could you help me?"

In a remarkably calm voice, she replied: "I'd love to... but I'm blind." Hearing this, I turned for support to her dog.

(This comes from watching too many episodes of *Lassie* growing up. "Go get help, girl, Timmy's fallen down the well!") Her ca-

nine companion, however, proved to be one short in the leg department.

I suspect he was named Lucky... or maybe Tripod. In the end, these unlikely rescuers bravely disentangled me, rounded up my errant dogs and summoned help. Then it was off to the hospital, where surgeons rebuilt my mangled limb with about six pounds of surgical steel.

I'm not sure if I learned anything from this adventure, but it did change me in one remarkable way... I can now attach fridge magnets to my forearm.

"CRUNCH! CRUNCH! CRUNCH!"

CHAPTER 18

You may already BE A WIENER

A S a respected, longtime member of the National Geographic Society, I am thrilled to announce I have solved one of the Great Mysteries of the Universe.

If you haven't already guessed, I am referring to a question that has long puzzled our greatest minds — why is Paris Hilton famous?

Ha ha ha! I am joking, of course. Some mysteries were never meant to be solved. (This would include Britney Spears and Ashlee Simpson.)

What I am trying to say here is that I had some spare time over the long weekend, and I used it to unravel the Mystery of the Missing Socks.

I am referring, of course, to single socks which, in my case, tend to disappear at the peak of ripeness.

Perhaps you think I am exaggerating the level of interest in missing socks. Well, perhaps — and I mean this in the best possible way — you are an idiot.

Consider this: A Google search for the words "missing socks" generates 4,090,000 hits. I have no idea what that means, but it can't be good.

There are legions of websites devoted to this phenomenon, some featuring polls allowing respondents to speculate on the fate of missing socks.

107

Leading theories include:

1) **The Sock Fairy steals them** (24 per cent)
2) **They become invisible** (14 per cent)
3) **They go to Brazil** (11 per cent)
4) **They are abducted by aliens** (nine per cent)

These theories, of course, are completely wrong.

I discovered this over the holiday weekend when, after walking the dogs, I carefully placed a pair of my finest sweatsocks on the floor.

(At my house, we have Magical Laundry Fairies that pick up stinky socks and put them in the clothes hamper. We also have fairies that restock the fridge and change the toilet paper roll.)

While standing, sockless, in the bathroom, I heard the sound of tiny, tentative steps sneaking into the bedroom. Peering into the room, I noticed our miniature wiener dog, Zoe, glancing around in what I can only refer to as a suspicious manner.

Then, without warning, she snatched one of the aromatic socks and, after casting a few more furtive glances, escaped with her prize.

With the stealth of a big jungle cat, I followed the sock thief to its lair, by which I mean a kennel in the living room, where I recovered no fewer than — I am not lying — SIXTEEN missing socks.

This is not the kind of behaviour one normally expects from your typical mild-mannered wiener dog, but, perhaps, we have all been fools.

I base this statement on a video clip I watched this week after a friend sent me a link to YouTube.com, the hugely popular video-sharing website.

The clip shows a lovely American family standing in a field proudly watching fireworks on July 4 when, suddenly, a brazen wiener dog darts out and steals their socks.

Ha ha ha! No, this wiener dog actually grabbed a lit Roman candle between its teeth and began madly dashing around, sending colourful fireballs careening at the now-screaming family members.

No one was injured, but clearly wiener dogs and flaming objects are a bad combination.

I am thinking here of General Edi, a 22-year-old Austrian dachshund whose owner credits his pet's long life to a daily diet of... cigarettes.

According to Ananova.com, General Edi has munched his way through 10 smokes a day for the last 17 years. Boasts his owner: "He eats the tobacco and the paper, then chews awhile on the filter before spitting it out."

Anyway, consider the sock mystery solved. In my next column I plan to reveal what happened to Jimmy Hoffa's body. I already have a suspect in mind.

CHAPTER 19

LOVE IS
STRANGE

IT'S officially spring, a time when even hardened columnists such as myself feel moved to relate heartbreaking stories of unrequited love.

So grab a few boxes of Kleenex because, fortunately for you, I have just such a heart-rending tale at my fingertips.

It's the story of Quentin, a lonely young fellow from Minnesota who moved to Winnipeg this summer, and, as young males will do, immediately began searching for "a little action."

But despite his Fabio-style golden locks and rippling muscles, Quentin just couldn't find that special someone to share his new life in Winnipeg.

Forlorn, he spent his days just kind of grazing and hanging around in the park. His friends and co-workers grew increasingly worried.

And then, as so often happens in stories such as this, it just happened — romance literally rolled into Quentin's life.

He awoke one recent morning and discovered he was deeply, madly, hopelessly in love — with a beautiful 45-gallon blue plastic water barrel.

Which is a little bit unusual, even when you consider that Quentin is a 650-pound Sichuan takin (an endangered species of golden-fleeced cattle native to western China) who makes his home at the Assiniboine Park Zoo.

I came across Quentin the Takin (pronounced Talk-inn) and his inanimate love interest recently during a special spring tour of the zoo with its amiable curator Dr. Bob Wrigley.

"He (Quentin) pushes it (his beloved barrel) the whole length of the exhibit," Wrigley said as the massive relative of the muskox gently nuzzled the battered container, which remained oblivious to his affections.

"You can see the barrel has taken quite a beating," Wrigley told me, heaving a sigh. "We'll have to get him a new barrel pretty soon. You'd think he'd get bored with this, but he just keeps going."

The soft-spoken curator noted Quentin hasn't been shy about displaying the intensity of his feelings for the barrel.

"It was pretty obvious to the public what was going on," he said. "The public would walk by and say, 'What the heck is that?'

"I feel sorry for the poor guy. I'm hoping to get a female for him this fall from a zoo in Minnesota. It would be much better for him than a barrel! There's only half a dozen zoos in North America that have these guys."

Looking on, zoo visitor Carmen Grant said she hopes Wrigley is successful in his bid to play matchmaker.

"Oh, the poor guy," Grant said of Quentin. "He's sniffing his barrel. He needs a mate. He's very cute!"

During our cruise around the zoo, it quickly became clear that Quentin wasn't the only one with love on the brain this spring.

"The increase in daylight stimulates all the animals into breeding," Wrigley explained. "There's just a flurry of excitement. We have

like supermodels

3) Stretching their wings, then tucking their heads under one wing

4) Battering nearby flamingos with their beaks.

1,200 animals of 380 species, so there's always something going on."

Over at the Tropical House, for example, things were definitely starting to get a little steamy.

We looked on as nine pink Caribbean flamingos unabashedly — and loudly — engaged in the following exotic courtship routine:

1) Fluffing their feathers and screeching like fighter jets

2) Flicking their heads from side to side

"They're trying to look attractive to the opposite sex," Wrigley shouted over the deafening din.

Before anyone gets too worked up, I will point out that we did not actually witness any flamingos getting beyond first base, and there is a sound scientific reason for this — flamingos are just a bit kinky.

"Flamingoes exist in large flocks," the curator noted. "To get sufficient sexual excitement, they need the presence of large numbers of other flamingos.

"Some zoos put a wall of mirrors in there to fool the flamingos into thinking there is twice the number. But we don't do that."

Still, spring fever was definitely hot and heavy in the Tropical House. For example, we spotted 13 baby bearded dragons (which are tiny and not all that scary) baking under a heat lamp. Nearby, the giant African land snail (not at all scary) had laid a batch of eggs and a huge Indian python (very scary) was preparing to lay eggs. I gave the snake a wide berth because I did not wish to appear too nosy.

Even the tortoises, Wrigley revealed, have gotten off to an unusually quick start this spring.

"Do you know how a tortoise mates?" I asked the curator.

"Why, yes!" he began.

Then, just as he was about to explain, I blurted: "Very s-l-o-o-o-o-o-w-l-y."

"Ha ha ha ha," Wrigley replied, although I strongly suspect he thought it was a pretty lame joke. He also did not agree that it would be fun to stick your hand in the piranha tank, so we moved on.

Another exciting spring development is the fact that senior citizens' thoughts are clearly turning to passion — at least at the city zoo.

The zoo's aging bald eagles, for instance, recently got together for some serious canoodling. "They caught us totally off guard," Wrigley beamed as we looked at the huge birds. "They're in their 40s and they're still sexually active. That's unheard of!"

"Yes," I politely told Wrigley. "Sex in your 40s... I hear that's pretty rare. Not that I'm an expert."

This seemed like a good time to move on to the Monkey House where — and this will be a shock — there has been plenty of monkey business.

"The lion-tailed macaques have had three babies," Wrigley said while a group of parent monkeys glared at us as we watched their tiny toddlers scuttling around the cage.

Elsewhere in the zoo, the caribou, elk and deer, which dropped their antlers in the winter, are now starting to sprout new horns for the spring.

"Having a BIG set of antlers is what REALLY impresses the female caribou," Wrigley sagely advised me.

As a person of the male gender, I firmly agreed. "Yes," I sniffed. "I imagine a sports car helps, too."

So that pretty much did it for my big day at the zoo, but at least I learned that, regardless of your species, love is still what makes the world go round.

Especially if you happen to be inside a barrel.

"
"Do you know how a tortoise mates?" I asked the curator.
"Why, yes!" he began.
Then, just as he was about to explain, I blurted:
"Very s-l-o-o-o-o-o-w-l-y."

BEWARE!
It's the Thing that Lurked in the Garage

IT was a dark and stormy weekend, and I was doing some important research on the couch when my wife suggested I might want to take part in a traditional spring activity.

"I'd love to, but I'm working right now," I informed her, remembering to put just a touch of sadness in my voice.

"You're reading the Travel Section," she felt compelled to point out.

"Yes, I was thinking about writing a column on Finland," I sniffed.

"I have a better idea," she said, unimpressed that I was "working" on the weekend. "I think you should look into cleaning the garage."

I squinted over the paper. "No problem," I said, agreeably. "I will definitely look into cleaning the garage."

119

I will not bore you with the rest of our discussion; the point is, a short time later, I found myself outside actually "looking into" our garage. It has been scientifically proven there are two kinds of men in the world, specifically:

> **"HONEY!!!" I yelled to my wife. "Can you come out here and look in the garage for a minute?"**

1 Men for whom garages are sacred temples, in which rakes are perfectly aligned on little hooks, gleaming power tools are lovingly arranged in alphabetical order on squeaky-clean workbenches, and freshly waxed cars sparkle like four-wheeled diamonds

2 Men such as myself, for whom garages are giant storage closets crammed to the rafters with mud-caked golf clubs, grease-covered things that at one time may have been functioning lawn mowers, cardboard boxes marked stuff and, judg-

ing by the smell, the remains of Jimmy Hoffa

As I stood there marvelling at my collection, my eye was drawn to a sudden and unexpected movement in the far corner.

And that's when I first saw "it." To tell the truth, I was not sure exactly what "it" was, but "it" was roughly the size of a basketball, a shadowy creature covered with blackish hair and moving in what I felt was an extremely suspicious manner behind an assortment of bikes and boxes at the back.

Fortunately, I knew exactly what NOT to do. I did NOT walk to the back of the garage and start moving things to get a better look. I have seen enough horror films to know that people who get too curious are eventually attacked by whatever is lurking in the shadows and their bodies are later discovered missing a great many medically important organs.

Fortunately, I also knew what I had to do. "HONEY!!!" I yelled to my wife. "Can you come out here and look in the garage for a minute?"

"There's... a THING... living in our garage!"

"What's wrong?" my wife asked after joining me in the driveway.

"There's... a THING... living in our garage!"

"What kind of THING?"

I held my hands apart to give her a feeling for its size. "It's big, kind of black, kind of hairy, and it gave me the distinct impression of having teeth."

"What kind of THING?"

My wife gave me a blank look. "It's probably a bunny," she said.

"Nuh-uh!" I replied, scowling to show how dumb the suggestion was.

By now, our daughter had joined us as we stood staring into the garage.

"What are you looking at?" she asked.

"Your dad saw a THING in the garage," my

121

wife snickered.

"What kind of THING?" my daughter demanded.

And that's when I heard what I can only describe as an annoyed, screeching sound. Suddenly, a dark shape darted out from behind a box and stood chattering in a menacing manner on top of a cluttered shelf.

"Look!" I bravely yelled, pointing at the baseball-sized creature.

"It's a squirrel," my wife and daughter snorted in unison before erupting into uncontrollable giggles.

"It's a BIG one," I tried to explain, but I don't think they heard me. As it turns out, there were, in fact, TWO squirrels, a gang, I told my family.

I pointed out it might be best for me to wait until after the unruly little rodents had moved out before trying to clean the garage.

"That's a good idea," my wife agreed. "They're probably looking for nuts."

"They're probably looking for nuts"

CHAPTER 21

WHO'S THE REAL KILLER?
Only the nose knows

I do not wish to sound overly morbid, but I know exactly what the police will think when they discover my body. "Look," one officer will say as they stare down at the bathtub, "He drowned himself!"

"Yes," his partner will agree, "But doesn't his hair look NICE???"

And he will be absolutely correct. But while the detectives are admiring the lustrous sheen of my "bouncing and behaving" hair, the real killer will sneak silently from the bathroom, pad down the hallway to the kitchen, sniff his food dish in a sullen manner and then saunter into the living room, where he will curl up in his favourite comfy chair and hope against hope that one of the nice police officers will decide to take him out for walkies.

125

... like a small furry animal has crawled on top of my head and died

I can explain. The problem is my hair, which is of the type that every morning, after an entire night flip-flopping in bed, becomes all smushed together into a kind of faux Mohawk, making it look like a small furry animal has crawled on top of my head and died.

This is why, first thing every day, I climb in the tub and slowly sink back under the water, feet sticking straight up, so I can wash my hair. Sadly, this hasn't been possible for the last few weeks because I tore my Achilles tendon and have been forced to wear

a) a cast that you cannot get wet; and
b) a Frankenstein-style boot that takes trained medical personnel approximately six hours to put on or take off.

Technically speaking, I could take a shower but this involves a process slightly more complicated than quantum physics and requires three industrial-strength garbage bags, two extra-large bath towels and roughly 3,482 metres of duct tape.

In one of those odd bursts of inspiration that usually come in the middle of the night — "Eureka! A DVD rewinder!!!" — I hit upon this brilliant plan:

1) Hobble into the bathroom on crutches;
2) Fill the tub until it is almost over-flowing;
3) Drop your robe on the floor;
4) Get down on all fours, lean w-a-a-a-a-a-a-y over the tub while resting your stomach on the edge, driving all the air out of your lungs in a sort of self-administered Heimlich manoeuvre;
5) Dunk your head under the water and, holding your nose with one hand, use the other to wash your hair.

Brilliant, right? Well, that's exactly what I've been doing. Unfortunately, there is — and you won't have seen this coming — a serious flaw with this plan, namely that when you are naked and you are dangling over the tub, your backside will be stuck up in what self-defence experts and most hair-stylists agree is AN EXTREMELY VULNER-ABLE POSITION.

This is not the kind of position you want to be in if, say, there happen to be any cyclists in the immediate area because chances are they will mistake you for a bike rack. Also, do NOT try this if you own a dog.

And so there I was the other day, washing

my hair in this "vulnerable position," when, unbeknownst to me, one of the dogs wandered in on the off chance I was scouring the tub and looking for biscuits.

You wildlife experts out there will know that your typical dog cannot resist greeting another dog by sticking his/her nose into their "personal region" and sniffing vigorously. To a dog, this is just "shaking hands."

Anyway, I do not remember precisely what went through my mind when, as I dangled over the tub with my head under water, SUDDENLY something cold and wet jabbed me in my defenceless personal region.

> **"**
> **SUDDENLY something cold and wet jabbed me in my defenceless personal region**

What I do remember is reacting with all the cool and calm you would expect from a trained humour columnist — I screamed (try this with your head under water), bolted upright, tipped over and hammered my head into the faucet at a speed I would describe as "space shuttttle re-entry."

All in all, I'm lucky to be alive. And that's why I am calling on the federal government to immediately order shampoo-makers to put this warning on every bottle: "ATTENTION, IDIOTS. DO NOT USE THIS PRODUCT WITH YOUR HEAD IN THE TUB AND YOUR BUTT IN THE AIR!"

" Sniffff... sniffffff

But if you insist on washing your hair in this manner, go ahead, knock yourself out. I'm not going to stick my nose into your business.

HERO

CHAPTER 22

Lassie, help...
GO GET THE CAT!

TODAY I'm going to recommend that we all begin a slow and steady panic over the fact the universe has apparently been turned upside down.

I'm referring to shocking reports of dogs acting like cats, cats acting like dogs and pet fish acting like pyromaniacs.

Some of these major stories may have slipped under your radar, but fortunately it's just the kind of news that captures my attention when I'm not sound asleep on the couch.

Let's begin with cats, which generally are deemed to be "independent" and "intelligent."

The very fact those words appear in quotation marks should tip you off that some observers consider cats to be "evil" or "not overly fond of people."

I would stress here that I am not talking about myself because I have no desire to be flooded with outraged letters on stationery boasting, "I (heart) my cat."

Anyway, you can imagine my surprise when I spotted this headline on an alarming Canadian Press story: "Hero cat saves child."

According to the story — which they insist is true — a pet cat named Mel-O prevented a nine-year-old Edmonton boy from having a diabetic seizure.

It seems the cat, which normally avoids people, crawled on the boy's bed and batted him awake just as his (the boy's) blood sugar fell to dangerously low levels.

"He had five minutes before he would have seized. He would have... slipped into a coma and died," the boy's mother said in praising the cat's heroics.

Some cruel observers might suggest this doesn't exactly fit with the traditional Cat Mission Statement, which includes:

1) **Being aloof**

2) **Hiding under beds and scratching people's legs**

3) **Sitting at busy intersections and encouraging dim-witted dogs to dart through traffic by saying: "Go ahead, Spike, you can make it"**

4) **Lurking around stairs to "accidentally" trip elderly rich widows who may have left them large sums of money in their wills**

Now that we have alienated a good 50 per cent of our pet-loving readers, we should immediately turn our attention to the big dog news, namely: "Designer dog burns down kitchen."

This is an even more alarming item because it involves a pet pup in Illinois causing about $70,000 damage by torching his owner's kitchen.

According to the *Chicago Sun-Times*, Skylar, a three-year-old "goldendoodle," started the blaze when he jumped on the stove to get some leftover pizza and somehow switched on a burner.

Skylar, a cross between a golden retriever and a poodle — and you just know that's not natural — had to be rescued by firefighters.

Now this story clearly conflicts with the accepted Dog Mission Statement which, when I last checked, looked like this:

1) **Barking at stuff**

2) **Piddling on stuff**

3) **Sniffing other dogs' personal regions**
4) **Rescuing people when their kitchens**

start on fire or when they are pinned under heavy objects. If you grew up watching Lassie, you know these hazardous events happen quite frequently

I would like to suggest we all start seriously fretting over this, but we don't have time.

We need to turn our attention to yet another alarming news story, specifically: "Fire blamed on pet fish."

According to an Internet news service, an English woman and her two daughters are lucky to be alive after one of their fish ignited a house fire.

The story describes how Kipper, an eight-inch catfish, sparked the fire by getting into a "fish fight" with a rival in their tank.

Apparently (see if you can follow along) some water slopped out of the aquarium, landed on an electric plug, sending a power surge up a light cable, burning the tank's plastic lid, which melted and dripped onto a leather sofa, which burst into flames. Got it?

I think we can all agree this definitely does not fit with the Fish Mission Statement, which clearly states... OK, maybe a helpful reader can write in to tell us all exactly what's in the Fish Mission Statement.

But the important safety point I'm trying to make here is that we can no longer sit back and rely on our trusty dogs and plucky tropical fish to rescue us when our homes suddenly erupt in flames.

No, pet owners, from now on you are going to have to rely on Mr. Whiskers to drag you to safety.

So, good luck with that.

Fish Mission Statement?

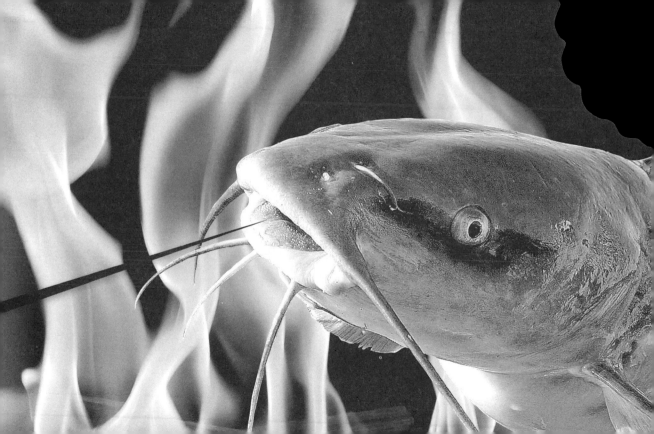

CHAPTER 23

If you think squirrels like motorists, **YOU'RE NUTS**

Grrrrrrrrrrrrrrrr...

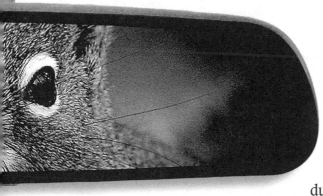

NOW that our lawmakers are moving to ban drivers from chattering away on cellphones, I think it's high time members of the motoring public called on the government to step up to the plate and outlaw an even greater menace plaguing our nation's highways.

As you have no doubt already deduced, I am talking about squirrels. I am raising this troubling issue today because of a recent horrifying and totally true squirrel-related vehicular incident involving my friend and colleague, Jeff de Booy, who is an extremely talented photographer and normally very cool and collected behind the wheel.

For a couple of years now, Jeff has been locked in an ongoing battle with legions of squirrels that have been gnawing their way into the foundation of his home. To beat back the invaders, Jeff purchased a rodent trap he has used to capture 19 squirrels, along with three birds, a neighbour's cat "and a large green frog, but not all at the same time."

Jeff's routine is to pop the caged squirrels into the back seat of his car and then, while en route to work, drop the offending rodents off at some attractive wooded area faaaaaaar away from his home.

This seemed to be working perfectly well for both Jeff and the squirrels until a few weeks ago, when my friend was happily motoring along and suddenly had to slam on the brakes because a car in front of him made an unexpected stop.

When he resumed driving, Jeff had the unmistakable feeling he was being watched, so he glanced into the rear-view mirror and there, staring back at him with a beady-eyed look of pure evil, was the reflection of one very angry squirrel.

I know what you are thinking here. You are thinking: "Ha ha ha. The cage obviously popped open, allowing the squirrel to escape, when your friend hit the brakes."

Anyway, the two stared at each other for several dramatic seconds until the squirrel, in a blinding flash of pent-up fury, began racing around the car, bouncing off the windows, the dashboard and, of course, Jeff's head.

I should point out that, as a professional newspaper photographer, Jeff is used to handling the intense pressure of deadlines and breaking news.

So he knew exactly what to do: He immediately stepped on the gas and slammed the car into the side of a building, killing himself and the squirrel.

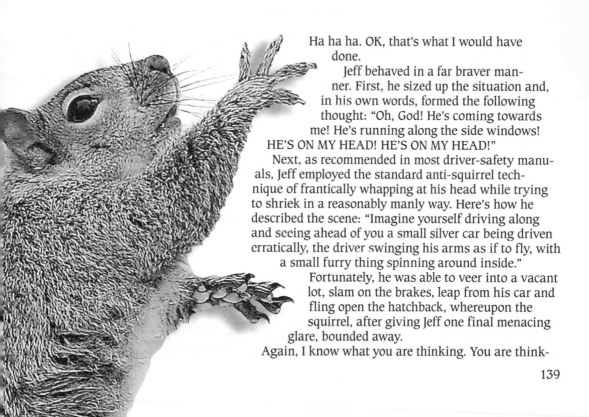

Ha ha ha. OK, that's what I would have done.

Jeff behaved in a far braver manner. First, he sized up the situation and, in his own words, formed the following thought: "Oh, God! He's coming towards me! He's running along the side windows! HE'S ON MY HEAD! HE'S ON MY HEAD!"

Next, as recommended in most driver-safety manuals, Jeff employed the standard anti-squirrel technique of frantically whapping at his head while trying to shriek in a reasonably manly way. Here's how he described the scene: "Imagine yourself driving along and seeing ahead of you a small silver car being driven erratically, the driver swinging his arms as if to fly, with a small furry thing spinning around inside."

Fortunately, he was able to veer into a vacant lot, slam on the brakes, leap from his car and fling open the hatchback, whereupon the squirrel, after giving Jeff one final menacing glare, bounded away.

Again, I know what you are thinking. You are thinking: "It is unfair to focus on a single isolated incident involving a rogue squirrel when the bulk of the squirrel population poses little or no threat to our nation's motorists."

Well, let me just say — and I mean this in the best way possible — you are deluded. Consider a story that recently appeared in the *New Jersey Star-Ledger* under this headline: "Flaming kamikaze squirrel ignites car."

According to this story, a buck-toothed New Jersey squirrel was gnawing on some overhead power lines that were connected to a transformer directly above a 2006 Toyota Camry.

We'll let the car's owner pick up the story: "The squirrel chewed through the wire, was set on fire and fell down directly to where the car was. The squirrel, on fire, slid into the engine compartment and blew up the car."

I would like to tell you the threat ends there, but I would be lying. I have just read a story on the BBC News website with this ominous headline: "Frozen squirrels pose car threat."

This story describes some of the more unique car insurance claims handled in recent months by U.K. insurer Norwich Union, including the following: "A frozen squirrel fell out of a tree and crashed through the windscreen onto the passenger seat."

What we find ourselves wondering now is whether these incidents are pure random chance or whether squirrels are banding together in a revolt against their human oppressors.

 ... **squirrels are banding together in a revolt against their human**

For now, if you find yourself trapped in a car with an enraged squirrel, I strongly advise you, at all costs, to remain calm.

Whatever you do, don't let them think you're nuts!

... revenge is sweet

CHAPTER 24

Day of drama, **JEALOUSY AND 'SNOODS'** at dog show

S USPENSE. Drama. Intrigue. Mystery. Anger. Jealousy. Terror.

Yes, you guessed it, we're at the dog show. It's 8 a.m. and already the tension is so thick you could cut it with a Milkbone.

Everywhere you look, pampered pets are being frantically primped, teased, snipped, brushed, combed, vacuumed and blow-dried.

It's kind of like a Beverly Hills salon just before the Academy Awards, except I don't think posh salons keep their clients in cages or provide them with a special sawdust-covered area to relieve pre-show jitters.

"It's a hobby but it's very competitive," explains Sonny Tougas, superintendent of the Northwinds Dog Show. "You can take two to four hours to prepare a dog for 2½ minutes of judging."

All the top dogs are here, including the semi-legendary Muldoon Dewitt Great One, a six-year-old Irish setter widely touted as the Wayne Gretzky of the dog world.

The Great One was flown into town for this three-day event, which is pretty much the Stanley Cup of dog shows.

Then, of course, there are some of the lesser lights. This is where I come in, or rather my six-year-old basset hound Cooper.

If Muldoon Dewitt Great One is the doggie Gretzky, Cooper is more or less the canine Vladimir Krutov, a former Russian hockey player known as "the Tank" who became famous during a brief NHL career for stuffing himself with hotdogs, potato chips and Slurpees before every practice.

On this day, however, there's just a little more pressure on Cooper than usual.

My wife — She Who Must Not Be Named — has

decreed that the moment Cooper's career in the show ring is over — ZOOM! — it's off to the vet's to have... "THE OPERATION!"

When she says this, she fixes me with a rather disconcerting look, which makes it clear that when my show career is over, I, too, will be expected to have THE OPERATION!

I realize female readers are probably pumping their fists in the air and thinking that my wife must be an extremely intelligent and just woman, while male readers are likely doubled over in sympathetic agony.

It seems my wife hasn't completely forgiven Cooper for a recent incident in which he ripped open a 20-pound sack of flour, ate about five pounds, then slurped down a gallon of water, transforming himself into a giant walking ball of glue.

The problem is Cooper's a basset hound. Yes, yes, they look pretty darned cute on those Hush Puppies shoeboxes, but in reality

they are land sharks, nature's Perfect Eating Machine.

Consider how Cooper psyched himself up for the big show: He knocked over our wiener dog's nine-pound bag of food, ate whatever was inside, then got his head stuck inside the bag and staggered around the kitchen like a drunken sailor, randomly crashing into chairs and cabinets.

I'm convinced that if space aliens were to observe our house for any length of time they'd report to their leaders that Earth is ruled by ravenous long-eared monsters that drink from the toilet.

Still, Cooper isn't a complete slouch. In fact, at one point this year he was technically rated the No. 18 basset hound in the nation.

I like to trot out that fact whenever people come over to our house and boast how their kids are going to Harvard Medical School or curing terrible diseases or doing wonderful unpublicized work for the poor.

I can only assume from the glazed looks on their faces that they are, in fact, deeply impressed.

Back at the convention centre, meanwhile, things are getting serious.

It's almost time to head into the ring and all the bassets are putting on their game faces and taking off their "snoods," brightly coloured headwraps that keep their ears from dragging on the floor. Dust bunnies on your ears is, of course, a serious faux pas.

As the hounds strut their stuff, the judge spends a good minute or so running his hands over every conceivable part of Cooper's anatomy. Checking for concealed weapons, I assume.

Sadly, this just isn't my dog's day.

Muldoon Dewitt Great One is heading for a date with destiny. Cooper, on the other hand, has a date with the vet.

I'm just glad he can't read this column. The less he knows, the better.

147

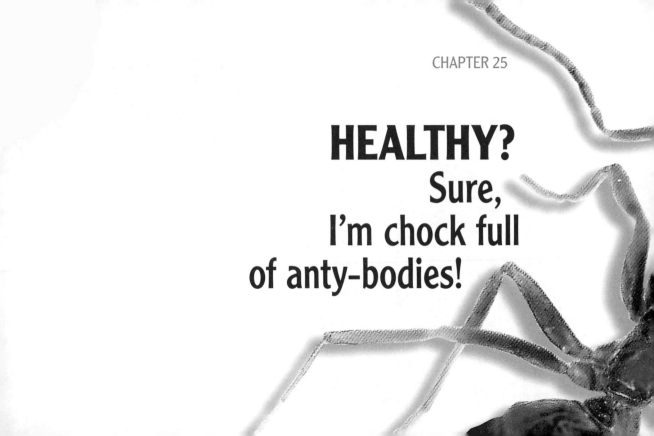

CHAPTER 25

HEALTHY?
Sure,
I'm chock full
of anty-bodies!

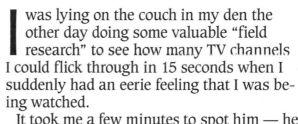

I was lying on the couch in my den the other day doing some valuable "field research" to see how many TV channels I could flick through in 15 seconds when I suddenly had an eerie feeling that I was being watched.

It took me a few minutes to spot him — he was crouched in the corner by the TV and staring at me in a menacing way that sent chills up my spine. Still, I was confident I could take him if it came to hand-to-hand combat, despite the fact he had at least six legs, whereas I currently have only two.

I do not mean to exaggerate the danger I was in, but as ants go, he was a big one. I would say this ant was easily the size of a regulation softball.

Normally, I know exactly how to handle hazardous situations such as this: I scream for my wife, who, under the terms of our marriage agreement, is obligated to handle any threats posed by things that can scientifically be described as "bugs."

I, on the other hand, am responsible for mice, lawyers and telemarketers, but that is not the point. The point is my wife was out shopping, so I was left to face the multi-legged intruder on my own.

Consequently, I slipped casually out of the den, moving slowly so as to suggest I was merely popping out for a snack, then raced to my computer desk to select an appropriately deadly weapon, namely the *Random House Dic-*

tionary of the English Language (Unabridged Edition), which is the size and weight of a small foreign car.

I planned to drop this on top of the ant while perched on the couch, but when I made my way back to the den, the ant was nowhere to be seen.

This was not good. I am not an entomologist (literally "someone who knows something about ants") but I do know that my den is not an appropriate environment for ants. The appropriate environment for ants is my backyard, the current composition of which breaks down as follows:

1) **Grass (six per cent)**
2) **Things left behind by my dogs (21 per cent)**
3) **Plastic**

garden ornaments pulverized by my lawn mower (38 per cent)
4) Anthills (79 per cent)

The key thing here is that you never just have ONE ant in your house. Ants are not what you call "loners." They travel in large, unruly gangs, so if you spot one ant, you can be fairly sure he is a "scout," an advance man for a huge and lethal invading force of ants hungry for human flesh.

You likely think I'm joking here, but you would not be laughing so hard if you had been with my wife and myself on the weekend when we went to see *Indiana Jones and the Kingdom of the Crystal Skull*, which includes a scene in which not one, but two entire Russian spies are consumed in a matter of seconds by man-eating ants the size and colour of Twizzlers.

So ants can be bad news. We are not on good terms with the ants in our yard, possibly because we have been trying to kill them. Ha, ha, ha. That was just a joke because all you "entomologists" out there know it is impossible to kill an ant, especially if you are trying to do this utilizing "green methods" (translation: "methods that do not work.")

For example, we initially tried to attack our ants via the popular technique of boiling them alive. This involves heating big buckets of water on your barbecue and then pouring them on the ants. The only problem with this is that (a) you end up pouring most of the boiling water on your legs; and (b) the ants seem to like it.

Ditto for most of the other environmentally friendly techniques. Here are some of the other ways we have tried to wipe out our ants:

1 COFFEE GROUNDS
Have you ever seen an ant on a caffeine high? They do not keel over; they just become amazingly perky and waggle their antennae like tiny airport employees trying to signal a jumbo jet.

2 BORAX
This is supposed to make the ants explode; what it actually does is make the ants incredibly clean.

3 VINEGAR
Ever had someone splash vinegar in your face? I'll bet you found it really annoying. Well, so do ants. The end result is you have a bunch of really angry ants who now smell EXACTLY like french fries!

4 BABY POWDER
I'm not joking. This is all over the Internet. In theory, you sprinkle it on their little pathways. The only good thing is that the ants now leave teeny-tiny footprints. It also reduces chafing.

So we can see the "green methods" are not all they are cracked up to be. What you need here is something more lethal, such as the "Flaming Polish Towel Method," which I did not make up.

I have here an actual news item out of Poland bearing the headline: "Pensioner destroys apartments to kill ants." The story states that a Polish senior named Marcin Bartosz, 74, was being driven crazy by an invasion of ants, and so, being a person of the male gender, he dumped several gallons of pesticide down a ventilation shaft where he lived.

Surprisingly, this didn't do much to eradicate the problem, so he moved on to the next logical step — throwing a burning towel down the shaft, which sparked an explosion that left the apartments in ruins and sent Mr. Bartosz to hospital with third-degree burns.

On the upside, the ants haven't bothered anyone since. I'm reluctant to try this drastic method myself, but I may not have any choice.

Because I definitely do not like the way that french fry is looking at me.

Doug's house is this way, guys...

CHAPTER 26

Oops!
SWEDEN
HAD AN
ACCIDENT ON
THE CARPET

SWEDEN

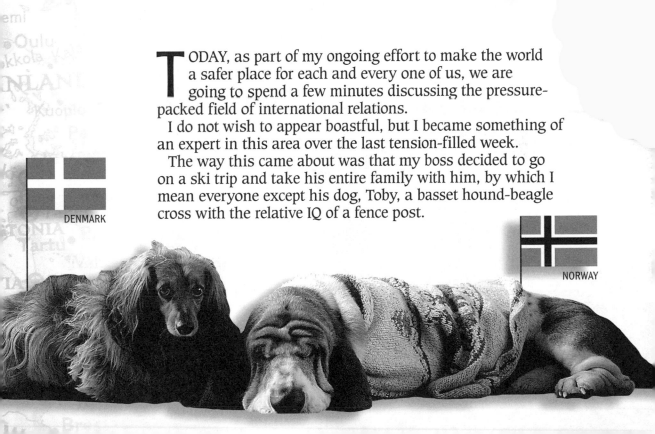

TODAY, as part of my ongoing effort to make the world a safer place for each and every one of us, we are going to spend a few minutes discussing the pressure-packed field of international relations.

I do not wish to appear boastful, but I became something of an expert in this area over the last tension-filled week.

The way this came about was that my boss decided to go on a ski trip and take his entire family with him, by which I mean everyone except his dog, Toby, a basset hound-beagle cross with the relative IQ of a fence post.

DENMARK

NORWAY

My boss pointed out that (a) Toby did not enjoy winter sports; and (b) my boss distinctly recalled that when I encouraged him to buy a dog in the first place, I apparently promised to personally look after it whenever he and his family went away on vacation, "no questions asked."

Regular readers will recall that, statistically speaking, I already have two dogs, so this means I have spent the past week attempting to maintain a fragile peace with three dogs living under the same roof.

If you do not currently have three dogs in your house, I have one question for you — can I come and live with you? Please? I'm very clean! Ha ha ha! I didn't think so. But your lack of hospitality is not the topic of today's column. Today's column is about how the social dynamics of having three dogs in the same house are very similar to the political dynamics among so-called friendly nations such as, say, Scandinavia.

For the purposes of this column, let's say my boss's dog (Toby) is Sweden, whereas my main dog, a basset hound named Cooper, is Norway, and my secondary dog, a miniature wiener dog named Zoe, represents the plucky nation of Denmark.

So when Sweden arrived for the big international meeting, it immediately triggered a border dispute by entering the bedroom of the United Nations (as represented by myself) and allowing its digestive system to explode on the carpet in front of the UN's clothes closet.

The UN's wife was not impressed by this diplomatic faux pas, which heightened tensions dramatically because Norway felt it had no choice but to retaliate by immediately occupying Sweden's kennel because it has a larger cushion than the one Norway usually sleeps on.

Denmark quickly entered the diplomatic brouhaha by racing around and yapping loudly at Sweden, until finally breaking off talks by running away and hiding under the UN's bed for several hours.

Do not get me wrong here. There have been periods of relative peace, such as right now when Sweden is snoring on the floor, Norway is curled up in a chair by the fireplace and Denmark is on top of the couch staring intently out the window, ready to bark in case any "rogue nations" happen to be going for a walk in the park with their owners.

But then, as always happens in the world of high-stakes diplomacy, something alters the balance of power. For example, if the

United Nations is sitting at the computer writing a column and foolishly decides to get up to go to the bathroom, the defence systems of all the "peaceful" nations immediately are thrown into high alert.

God forbid that, while en route to the bathroom, the UN decided to give Denmark a biscuit and Sweden and Norway were left to go hungry.

Another issue escalating tensions is Sweden's inexplicable efforts to "dominate" Denmark by staging unsolicited "assaults" on Denmark's (how shall we phrase this) undefended rear perimeter.

These sneak attacks only confuse Denmark, which refuses to retaliate even though the UN thinks this would be a really good idea.

Most annoying of all, in the UN's view, is that when the smallest nation (this would be Denmark) steals stinky socks from the floor in the UN's bedroom and stockpiles them in her kennel, all the other nations, none of whom had previously shown the slightest interest in socks, feel threatened and respond by trying to establish sock superiority in their own kennels.

To say nothing of the fact that Sweden, shortly after arriving at the peace talks, immediately captured Denmark's favourite stuffed toy sheep and ripped out its fluffy insides, which were then scattered throughout most of western Europe, as represented by our living room.

I am pleased to report, however, that the "balance of power" will soon be restored because Sweden's family is coming home soon.

But the price of world peace is constant vigilance, so if you'll excuse me, I have to run because, unless Denmark and Norway go outside right away, there is going to be an "international incident" at the backdoor.

And the UN definitely does not want to clean that up.

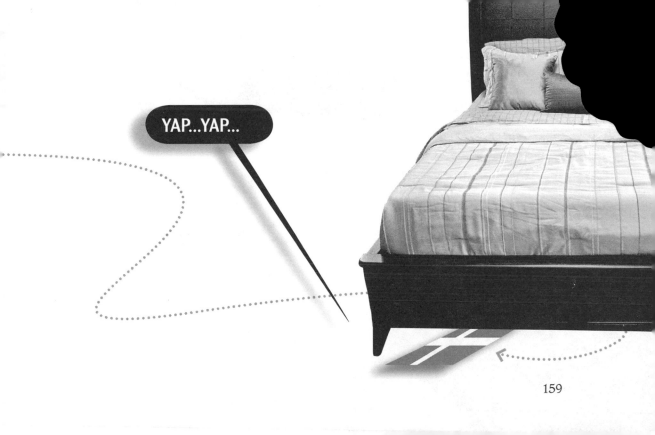

159

CHAPTER 27

"Hello ant...

Feeling antsy?
WELCOME TO THE BUG HOUSE!

Go away Grasshopper!

NOTE TO READERS:
Today, in place of my usual column,
I thought I would present a fable in hopes
of teaching us all a valuable moral lesson...
and then spend the rest of the weekend
sitting in my backyard drinking cold beer.
Thank you.

Doug Speirs

ONCE upon a time — which is the way all the best stories start — there was a Very Lazy Grasshopper who worked as a newspaper columnist in a wonderful land far, far away.

This was a very friendly, intelligent grasshopper — and, from what I hear, quite good-looking in an 80-pound overweight, kind of middle-aged way — but whenever the sun was shining, he had a very hard time keeping his mind on his work.

161

One extremely hot and humid summer day — for the sake of this story, we'll call it Friday — the Very Lazy Grasshopper just couldn't come up with an idea for his hugely popular column, In The Bug House.

"Oh no!" Grasshopper thought to himself, "I have spent all week playing and playing in the hot sun, and now I have nothing to write about."

Feeling terribly sorry for himself, the Very Lazy Grasshopper looked around the newsroom, which was packed mainly with ants of the hard-working, down-to-business, industrious variety.

Suddenly, Grasshopper got an idea. "I know!" he said quietly, "I will ask the ants to help me."

And so he did, casually hopping over to the ant busily working at the desk next to his cubicle.

"Hello, Ant," Grasshopper said politely.

"Go away, Grasshopper!" the ant scolded, angrily. "I am much too busy to waste time talking to a big green distraction like you."

"But I thought we could hop over to Starbucks together," Grasshopper said. "If I write about them, maybe they will send me lots of free stuff."

"NO!" said the ant, giving his antennae an annoyed waggle. "You should get down to work."

But Grasshopper didn't give up. He hopped over to another ant on the other side of the busy newsroom.

"Hello, Ant," Grasshopper said, thinking how helpful it was that all the ants had the same first name. "I was just wondering... "

But the ant cut him off. "Go away, Grasshopper!" the ant roared. "You just want me to say something funny so you can use it in that imprudent column of yours."

> You should get down to work.

> **I am much too busy to waste time talking to a big green distraction like you.**

"That's not true," Grasshopper replied, trying to sound offended. "And, by the way, how do you spell imprudent?"

But the second ant just gave him a frosty look, so Grasshopper bounced away to a third ant who made the mistake of looking up from his desk.

"Hello, Ant," Grasshopper began, "I spent too much time playing in the sun, and now I have nothing to write about."

The third ant had heard this story before. "Look, Grasshopper, just go and do what you always do — write something about your obnoxious teenagers."

"That's a good idea," Grasshopper chirped, "but they haven't done anything really bad lately. Mind you, I read about a teenager in a German hospital who unplugged his neighbour's life-support machine because he said the noise was, and I quote, 'getting on his nerves.'"

"Is that a true story?" the ant asked, knowing Grasshopper had a terrible reputation for fibbing.

"Yes," Grasshopper sniffed, again trying to sound offended. "I read it in an Associated Press article."

163

"Well, maybe you should mention that in your column so people won't think you are making it up," the ant advised.

"Good idea," Grasshopper said.

And with that bit of advice, Grasshopper merrily hopped back to his messy desk and started typing and typing until, finally, after several minutes of hard work, he had a column.

Then Grasshopper took his column and sidled — he could sidle very quickly for an insect — over to a senior editor, who happened to be a large beetle.

The editor read the column quickly and harrumphed. "This is pretty stupid, even for you," the beetle told Grasshopper.

"What do you mean?" Grasshopper asked, sadly.

"Well," said the beetle, "It doesn't even have a proper ending."

"I know," said Grasshopper, smiling. "That's the best part of all!"

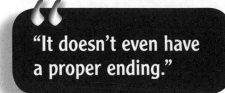

"It doesn't even have a proper ending."

164